What people are saying about
Stay the Course . . .

Pastor Choco's new book, *Stay the Course,* prompts us to anchor ourselves on the uncompromising Word of God. Many times we allow the world to dictate our faith, beliefs, and values, but we must always remember who we are in Christ. With piercing insights, gripping stories, and sound biblical principles, this book helps men and women, young and old, rich and poor, find and follow God's path for their lives.

Mark Batterson
New York Times best-selling author of *The Circle Maker*
Lead Pastor of National Community Church,
     Washington, D.C.

We live in a culture that is wandering farther from truth. My friend, Pastor Choco De Jesús, reminds us that God's Word remains true in our ever-changing world. In *Stay the Course,* he combines biblical principles with practical solutions to bring a vital message of hope to a drifting culture.

John Bevere
Best-selling author of *Good or God?, The Bait of Satan,*
     and *Relentless*
Minister and Cofounder of Messenger International

Not even five minutes into reading *Stay the Course: Finding Hope in a Drifting Culture,* I found my head nodding and my heart gripped by the powerful words of author and much-beloved pastor, Wilfredo "Choco" De Jesús.

It's no secret that this nation is in drift-mode, swirling farther and farther downstream from the solid foundation of biblical truths and values. Many of us cringe when we see those we love, even within the church, being swept away by this strong undercurrent. And at times, if we are honest, we feel the tug on our own souls and wonder if we'll be able to keep our footing against the prevailing cultural drift. Using relatable real-life stories, rich scriptural exposition, and relevant discussion questions, the author reminds us that if we know who our God is, and who we are in Him, we don't have to be part of that downward drift.

Pastor Choco has his finger on the pulse of current cultural realities, but his ear is pressed against God's chest, listening to the Father's heart. In *Stay the Course*, he shares this hope-birthing, divine heartbeat with the rest of us who don't want to be drifters. I, for one, am listening.

Dr. Jodi Detrick
Speaker, former columnist for *The Seattle Times*
Author of *The Jesus-Hearted Woman: 10 Leadership*
        Qualities for Enduring & Endearing Influence

Pastor Choco De Jesús is a captivating, insightful communicator, and his newest book, *Stay the Course*, is a welcome must-read. Describing the powerful cultural currents that impact followers of Jesus today, he offers clarity and refreshing honesty about our very human responses in times of troubling change. This book is a bold, practical call for the church to engage the people and issues in our culture . . . rather than drift off-course or run away. With insight and courage, Pastor Choco invites us to live with Jesus-inspired compassion and practice his presence with confidence in who we are as children of God. Weaving God's Word with stories of everyday lives, *Stay the Course* inspires, challenges, and informs. What a gift from a great pastor's heart for this prophetic moment in time!

Beth Grant, Ph.D.
Representative of the Executive Presbytery for the
        Assemblies of God
Co-director of Project Rescue
Author of *Courageous Compassion: Confronting Social*
        Injustice God's Way

In Pastor Choco's new book, *Stay the Course*, we learn how to keep our Christian perspective in a constantly changing world. Today we are witnessing the powerful undercurrents of history as our culture's morals and values shift. However, God's presence, truth, grace, and power haven't changed at all! Pastor Choco passionately reminds us to follow God's best by remaining focused on God's direction for our lives. This book is a must-read for all Christians.

Pastor Chris Hill
The Potter's House of Denver

A young married student I pastored was permanently blinded from a tragic auto accident. She could have given up on life, but she did not. She wrote poetically, "If I should quit, how could I face myself and place so many Scriptures on the shelf? A quitter or a conqueror I can be, and God has left the choosing up to me." As I read Pastor Choco's book and his admonition to *Stay the Course*, I'm reminded of her insight. Truly, God has left the choosing up to us. Through Scripture, personal stories, and illustrations, Pastor Choco urges us to go forward resolutely in our walks with Jesus, to avoid giving up or giving in to the adverse circumstances that come our way. *Stay the Course* will encourage many thousands and will prove to be a powerful resource to individuals and those who use it in group settings.

Dr. George O. Wood
General Superintendent, The Assemblies of God

Pastor Choco De Jesús is one of those rare voices in our day that points us to the true source of strength, peace, and hope for our generation. With a gracious yet uncompromising wisdom, he presents truths that cut against the grain of where our culture is heading.

Chrissy Cymbala Toledo
Author of *Girl in the Song*

In *Stay the Course*, Pastor Choco shares a transforming message that combines biblical wisdom and pragmatic faith, a message that helps us navigate the restless waters of a changing and confusing culture. It is a message that will challenge us to find and follow our "true north" and confront the challenges of a society drifting away from God. He encourages us to look ahead with truth that liberates and grace that heals. For those who have faith in God, we are assured that he has a clear direction we can follow without hesitation. As we follow him, we become a lighthouse of hope for the world.

Danilo Montero
Contemporary singer, author, and pastor

"To respond to the drift in our culture, we need a clear identity and a compelling purpose."

With this sentence Pastor Wilfredo "Choco" De Jesús invites us to define ourselves. Only then will we be able to be the answer our world needs. As a person who has been standing in the gap for my country of Puerto Rico, I encourage everyone to read *Stay the Course* so we can understand the context of the culture where we share the gospel of Jesus Christ. With the authority Pastor Choco has earned, and because of his career of being an influence in the nation, he shares concrete steps to help us confront our decadent culture so it doesn't keep drifting away.

Apostle Wanda Rolon
Pastor, author, and founder of Tabernacle of Worship and Restoration La Senda Antigua
President of Wanda Rolon Int'l Ministries and Christian Television Network International (CTNi)

Identity, destiny, and love. These three powerful words define the central concepts of the message God wants to convey to this generation through the writing of Pastor Choco. With wisdom and passion, he gives us the hope, courage, and resources to succeed in times of uncertainty, confusion, and anguish. *Stay the Course* is a lighthouse for all who seek to fulfill God's purposes.

Apóstol Edwin Álvarez
Senior Pastor, Comunidad Apostólica Hosanna

After reviewing the social, historical, and cultural evolution of the United States and the drift away from Christianity, Pastor Choco presents a biblical path to stay connected to the will of God. As we are anchored in God's Word, we won't be deceived by the temptations to drift from God and engage in destructive behaviors that harm the spiritual life of believers and their families.

Make no mistake: there are many dangers in our culture today, but Pastor Choco gives us spiritual and practical principles to help us relate to difficult people, adverse circumstances, temptations, and afflictions. With courage and hope, we will make good decisions to "stay the course."

Abel Flores
General Superintendent of Mexico, Assemblies of God

STAY THE
COURSE

FINDING HOPE IN
A DRIFTING CULTURE

CHOCO DE JESÚS

ISBN: 978-0-9973372-2-8

Published in the United States by Baxter Press, Friendswood, Texas

Printed in the United States

We dedicate this book to our beloved children,
Alex, Yesenia and Papito.
Always remember who you are.
Love, Papi & Mami

CONTENTS

CHAPTER 1

SIGNS OF DRIFT

Many of us feel stress and get overwhelmed
not because we're taking on too much,
but because we're taking on too little
of what really strengthens us.

—MARCUS BUCKINGHAM

Wherever we turn today, we find people who are afraid and angry. Their lives seem out of control, and their core values are rapidly eroding. In my interactions with people inside the church and outside, the powerful and the powerless, I hear all of them make similar remarks:

"People are talking out of both sides of their mouths. I don't know who to trust anymore!"

"With all the violence, I don't know if I'm safe in my own house."

"I worry about my kids' future."

"Why are we letting all these people into our country? They're taking our jobs, and some of them may be terrorists."

"Everybody needs a gun. At least I need one!"

"Can I ever find a good job, one I really enjoy?"

"Is it worth getting married? It costs so much, and many marriages don't work out."

"Will I have enough money to retire when it's my time?"

"What if I get really sick? Can I even afford the medicine and treatment I'll need? Will the healthcare system be there for me?"

"Nobody seems to care about me or what I value any longer. Either the culture has moved or I have, but something's really wrong."

"Is the church going to do anything about the weakening of our country's values?"

IT'S NOT JUST YOU

Some of us might assume that our concerns are only personal, but a glance at the news reveals that many Americans are afraid their security is slipping away. Recent surveys by both Gallup and the Barna Group reveal disturbing shifts in our culture. In the span of only a few years —the blink of an eye in cultural history—their surveys found:

- The number of Americans who support same-sex marriage has risen from twenty-seven percent to sixty percent in about a decade.[1]

- Correspondingly, four out of ten Americans cite worries over the loss of religious freedom.

- Based on a set of fifteen beliefs and behaviors, forty-four percent of Americans can be described as "post-Christian."

- In frustration, seven out of ten Americans today want political leaders who have clear, bold stances on issues that
  concern them. Of those who responded, this criterion for
  leadership is far more important than character or political
  experience.

- Many women feel isolated and vulnerable. Only seventeen
  percent of women report they feel "very" supported by
  their faith community. Consequently, many feel relationally
  distant from other believers.[2]

How did we get here? Young adults have grown up during
a time of rapid cultural changes, but those shifts began long
before they were born. Older Americans have witnessed a series
of events that have led us to this point. The prosperity of the
post-World War II years created a tsunami of change as memories of The Great Depression and the war quickly faded in the
rearview mirror. In *New Rules*, Daniel Yankelovich describes
how our culture moved from *self-sacrifice* before and during
World War II to *self-indulgence* in the decades after the war.[3]
People were deprived for a long time, and suddenly, they had
the opportunity to have it all! Modern advertising (think of *Mad
Men*) made big promises. Before, ads simply described how a
product or service worked, but then ads for beer, banks, and
cars (and every other imaginable product) began to promise
benefits of popularity, financial security, close friendships,
peace, freedom, and sexual attraction. Over-promising became
completely normal.

With increased income, parents had enough money for
their children to go to college. Until that point in our nation's
history, the vast majority of young people received, at best, a

high school education and then went to work on family farms or in their communities, remaining geographically close to their parents and grandparents. Suddenly, far more high school graduates had the opportunity to go to college. Moving away from home brought more freedom to experiment with lifestyle choices they wouldn't have dreamed of trying if they lived at home.

The excitement and optimism of the postwar years soon became clouded by the harsh realities of the Cold War with the Soviet Union, the close call of the Cuban Missile Crisis, and the violence against leaders of the Civil Rights movement. Shockingly, President Kennedy was assassinated, and a few years later, Martin Luther King, Jr. and Robert Kennedy were slain. The Vietnam War tore America apart, and Watergate shattered trust in our political leaders. Meanwhile, the Supreme Court ruled in a landmark 1973 case that abortion is legal in America. The 60s and early 70s were traumatic for America, but even during those tumultuous times, we put a man on the moon.

After those difficult years, we experienced a measure of peace and prosperity again. The generation born after the war, the Boomers, became self-absorbed and were dubbed "the me generation." A sexual revolution and the prevalent use of drugs swept America.

In the 80s and 90s, periods of prosperity and economic downturns dominated the news, yet America seemed safer than ever—especially after the Berlin Wall fell in 1989 and the subsequent collapse of the Soviet Union.

But then the events of September 11, 2001 shattered our sense of security. For those who lived through that day, the memories are as strong as Pearl Harbor or Kennedy's death was for earlier generations. America entered controversial wars in the Middle East. At home, gay marriage, which was unthinkable only a decade before, was validated by several states and then the Supreme Court. In recent years the issues have multiplied: immigration, refugees from the war-torn Middle East and turmoil in Latin America, police violence, and mass shootings. We now live with constant news about the dangers of terrorism, certainly abroad, but increasingly in our communities.

For young and old alike, it feels like our nation is coming apart at the seams!

Only in a world where faith is difficult can faith exist.

—PETER KREEFT

FOUR RESPONSES

We can identify four distinct responses to the changes in culture: accommodate, oppose, withdraw, or engage.[4] Sometimes we see all four in a single family. Let's examine these.

Some people *accommodate* change.

For these people, tolerance is the highest virtue. They don't want anyone to be superior to anyone else, so they accept every lifestyle and belief as equally valid.

Accommodators look at the shift in attitudes toward gay marriage (or guns, immigration, the use of force by police, or any other important cultural change), and they say, "It's no big deal. Everyone deserves fair treatment. And besides, it's not right to judge anyone! We need to keep in step with the culture. We need to go along to get along."

Some people fiercely *oppose* change.

This second group has the opposite reaction: when threatened by change, they see proponents of the other side as enemies who must be defeated, not reasonable people who have a different opinion. Even small shifts in society are seen as potential major losses because: "If you give an inch, they'll take a mile!"

These people oppose change because they are terrified that their way of life is going to be taken away—or worse, it has already been stolen from them. They only listen to friends or commentators who reinforce their fears and enflame their anger. Those who might offer an alternate voice of reason are considered fools and pawns of the opposition.

Some people *withdraw* to protect themselves.

This group assumes, "What's the use? My voice means nothing in the big debates about immigration, gun control, racial conflicts, or same-sex marriage. Those issues (and many others) are far too complex. And anyway, I don't want to get in the line of fire between people who are so angry!"

If someone corners them and demands a stated opinion, they shake their heads and say, "Oh, I don't know. That's beyond me." They believe not having an opinion protects them from getting caught in the fight between opposing forces. Many of them don't watch the news because, they've concluded, "It's too depressing."

These three reactions to cultural drift may seem completely good and right, but they undermine our identity as strong, compassionate, wise children of our heavenly King. For instance, those who accommodate change lose the sharp edge of truth.

When tolerance is overvalued, behaviors that were called "sin" a generation ago become acceptable topics for sitcoms today. Those who oppose change can lose their sense of grace, love, and mercy for those who disagree with them. And those who withdraw too quickly from intense debates and dialogs lose their God-given opportunities to represent him in a lost and confused world. So we will turn our attention to the fourth way to respond to the complexity and chaos of modern culture:

We can *engage* change with a beautiful blend of truth, grace, and purpose.

Jesus calls us to be "in the world but not of the world" (John 17:13-18) and to be "salt and light" to the people around us (Matt. 5:13-16). With this identity and perspective, we interact with people with truth and grace—not affirming their sins because we're afraid of being labeled judgmental, not harshly condemning them, and not withdrawing from them because interaction requires more than we want to give. Rather, in our engagement with people, we follow the example of Jesus. He moved toward the outcasts and the marginalized, and he touched the lepers and cared for those who were possessed by demons. He wept with those who lost loved ones, and he felt genuine sorrow when others chose a different path. He stood up against injustice, and he boldly faced the religious leaders who despised him for loving the unlovely.

Jesus lived a simple, humble life, but he wasn't threatened by scarcity. He trusted his Father to provide for him in every way. Jesus wasn't consumed by power, prestige, and popularity, so he didn't dissolve into self-pity when those things were taken from him. He had a strong confidence in his Father and his Father's will for him.

Every day, you and I have choices about how we respond to our culture. Most times it would be much easier for me to avoid difficult conversations and just go along with the pressure to accept same-sex marriage as the new normal . . . to look the other way when gun violence destroys another life and another family . . . to give up on the fight against abortion. Choosing to engage requires a lot from me! As I watch the people in our community and our church respond, withdrawal seems to be the most common response of all. I've seen, though, that these three unhelpful responses isolate us, diminish our impact, and hurt God's reputation.

Those who engage with wisdom, courage, and kindness need to set limits on what they're willing to accept. They sometimes have to draw clear lines and go no further. When the *New York Times* interviewed me about the recent cultural shift in our nation and our courts to accept same-sex marriage, they cited the Pew Research Center's findings that only 27 percent of white evangelicals support same-sex marriage and 70 percent oppose it. In other words, among Bible-believing Christians, the shift has been minimal. I explained, "In 2,000 years of Christian history, the church has often been at odds with the culture." This is not an issue that has shades of gray. I continued, "We're prepared to go to prison, or whatever occurs, but the church cannot change.[5] God has given us a clear path, and we need to stay the course.

I believe God wants me—and he wants you—to engage the demanding people and difficult issues in our culture. In my role as a pastor and community leader, I've had a lot of practice, but I still have to remember to look closely at how Jesus related to the helpless and the powerful, those who loved him and those who hated him. He tailored his response to each person, but always with the appropriate measures of gentleness and toughness.

God calls me to engage like Jesus, and he calls you to engage like him, too.

When we grasp our identity "in Christ," we realize we belong to another king and a different kingdom. Because our hopes are in that kingdom, we aren't shattered or surprised when this earthly kingdom is shaken. And we don't withdraw. We aren't remote or distant from the people around us. Our confidence gives us security so we can be fully engaged in knowing them, loving them, and representing our king to them.

Storms draw something out of us that calm seas don't.

—BILL HYBELS

Most people—including many Christians—are putting their hopes in the earthly kingdom. They expect their elected officials to lead them to the promised land of security and prosperity, and they are shocked when political promises don't work out as they expected. Jesus is, indeed, a sovereign and powerful king, but his reign and his purposes are very different from what most of us expect.

New Testament scholar N.T. Wright observes that Jesus came just as it had been predicted, but not at all the way people expected. The first century Jews, including the disciples, had to expand their concept of the God who became king. In *Simply Jesus*, Wright explains:

They were looking for a builder to construct the home they thought they wanted, but he was the architect, coming with a new plan that would give them everything they needed, but within quite a new framework. They were looking for a singer to sing the song they had been humming for a long time, but he was the composer, bringing them a new song to which the old songs they knew would form, at best, the background music. He was the king, all right, but he had come to redefine kingship itself around his own work, his own mission, his own fate.[6]

As we examine the responses of the people to Jesus, we'd have to conclude he was a big disappointment for most of them. He didn't overthrow the Romans after his "triumphal entry" into Jerusalem. He rode on the back of a donkey's colt with palm branches spread in front of him, not on a white stallion with swords flashing and trumpets blaring. He confused many people then, and he still confuses a lot of people. He simply doesn't do what we expect him to do.

A CLEAR IDENTITY, A COMPELLING PURPOSE

When I traveled to Burkina Faso, a nation north of Ghana on the Ivory Coast of Africa, I had the privilege of meeting with the king in his palace. I was ushered into the room where he sat, but I was instructed not to look directly at him. I was told to talk only to his aide, who would relay my words to him. When he replied, he talked to his aide, who then told me what the king said. We followed this odd protocol even though he was sitting just a few feet away.

Soon after we began, I told the aide, "Tell your king I am an ambassador of the kingdom of heaven."

When the aide repeated my words, the king broke tradition. He looked directly at me and said, "Would you pray for me?"

Suddenly, the formal, distant relationship dissolved into warmth and trust. I put my hands on him and prayed God's blessings on him. He then invited me on a tour of his private rooms in the palace, including a room of sports memorabilia. Later I learned he rarely invites anyone into that room. At the end of our tour, he had a picture taken of us. This, too, is a rare honor for a visitor.

Why did God give me that kind of access to this man? Only because I wasn't intimidated by his power and authority. I represented my King.

I try to live in this realization every day in every interaction. My King is still alive. He's compassionate and sovereign. This reality gives me peace when the world seems to be falling apart around me, and it lets me tap into the timeless wisdom of God when I face discouraging challenges. When I see how Jesus bent down to care for the poor and forgotten people of his day, I'm filled with compassion for the helpless men and women in our community. When I look at how he stood up against abuse and oppression, I feel his strength in my soul to speak out boldly to correct injustice today.

Make no mistake: the world is changing, and the culture is drifting away from the values we've held dear for generations. We live in a challenging age, but no more challenging than the first century when Rome ruled the world and Christians were often a persecuted minority. They trusted God for wisdom and courage to face economic loss and government opposition, and the church prospered because of their faith. Difficulties and threats are dividing lines in the lives of believers: we either go deeper into the reality of our King's love and purpose, we give up on him, or we blindly fight back against the tide that threatens us. God has called us to respond with truth *and* grace, not one or the other.

To respond to the drift in our culture, we need a clear identity and a compelling purpose. When the people of God were slaves in Egypt, they were physically, emotionally, and spiritually empty. For over four centuries, it seemed God had abandoned them, and their masters treated them harshly. But God appointed and empowered Moses to step into their pain and bring them out of bondage. As they left Egypt and miraculously crossed the Red Sea to escape certain death at the hands of the Egyptian army, they were a collection of freed but broken individuals. They had a leader, but their culture had been shattered by 400 years of oppression.

In the desert, God gave them two elements that formed their new identity: law and love. On Mt. Sinai, God showed up in awesome power and gave Moses the Ten Commandments. They now had God's laws, his commands, and the expectations of how they would relate to him and to each other. But that's not all. God also gave them detailed instructions for how to build the tabernacle. There, God's presence dwelled with the people, and their sacrifices regularly reminded them of God's forgiveness of their sin. God's beloved people, then and now, need both law and love to form and appreciate their identity. Law and love, truth and grace: these give us a sense of *who* we are, but even more, they loudly proclaim *whose* we are.

We belong to the Creator, the King, and the Savior of the world. God created the vast expanse of the universe, 13.6 billion light years across. (Each light year is six trillion miles.) He is more powerful and majestic than anything we can imagine, and the psalmist wonders how we could possibly matter to him:

> GOD, brilliant Lord,
>   yours is a household name.

I look up at your macro-skies, dark and enormous,
    your handmade sky-jewelry,
Moon and stars mounted in their settings.
    Then I look at my micro-self and wonder,
Why do you bother with us?
    Why take a second look our way?
    (Ps. 8:1, 3-4, MSG)

Daniel and Paul both demonstrated an unshakable commitment to God's purposes, even in the most difficult cultural conditions. We may think we have it tough in America, but Daniel served God with dignity and strength as an exile under Nebuchadnezzar, a repressive Babylonian king. Instead of feeling sorry for himself because he was so far from home and his captors had destroyed his land, Daniel saw his situation as an opportunity to represent God to a pagan king and a godless nation.

Success is not final, failure is not fatal: it is the courage to continue that counts.

—WINSTON CHURCHILL

Centuries later, Paul was a Jewish leader who was hostile toward Jesus and anyone who followed the Messiah. After Jesus met him on the road to Damascus, Paul's life was turned around and upside down. The angry, defiant man became a humble servant of God; the man who had abused others rejoiced that God considered him worthy to suffer for Christ's sake. Paul was later harassed, beaten, and imprisoned by a series of enemies, Jewish and Roman. Through it all, his purpose was never shaken or diluted. If anything, it became even stronger. On his last trip to Jerusalem, when he knew he would be falsely accused and imprisoned for his faith, Paul told his friends, "I consider my life worth nothing to me; my only aim is to finish the race and complete the task the Lord Jesus has given me—the task of testifying to the good news of God's grace" (Acts 20:24).

Paul was an optimist, but not a fool. He understood that suffering, and even persecution for our faith happens to those who are committed to follow Christ. We contain the matchless grace of God, but we are only clay pots, easily broken. Paul explained his perspective to the Corinthians:

> But we have this treasure in jars of clay to show that this all-surpassing power is from God and not from us. We are hard pressed on every side, but not crushed; perplexed, but not in despair; persecuted, but not abandoned; struck down, but not destroyed. We always carry around in our body the death of Jesus, so that the life of Jesus may also be revealed in our body. (2 Cor. 4:7-10)

What is our purpose in life? If we expect God to give us perfect peace and prosperity, to right all the wrongs and make our lives comfortable —right now!—we haven't been reading the Bible very carefully. Misplaced expectations inevitably lead to inadequate responses to life's difficulties. If our purpose is to represent the King of glory all day every day, we won't be surprised when he calls us to be kind instead of angry, to be bold instead of weak, to die to our selfish desires so the life of Jesus can shine through us.

That's how Daniel found strength to walk with God in a foreign land, and that's how Paul kept his head on straight when others wanted to chop it off!

We live between "the already" and "the not yet" of God's promises. He has given us "precious and magnificent promises" of forgiveness, the Spirit's presence and power, and a clear sense of purpose in this life, but the complete fulfillment of all of God's promises won't come until the new heaven and new earth. When that day arrives, all wrongs will be made right, all sins left behind, all hurts healed, all errors corrected, and the family of God will finally be united in his loving presence and under his rule. But that day isn't today. For now, we need to dive deep into our identity as God's dear children, following his law and basking in his love. And we need to refine and pursue God's purpose to make us salt in a decaying world and light in a dark culture—not to expect lives of complete comfort and ease. That's what it means to belong to him.

Our task every day is to remember who God is and who we are. My daughter Alex is a beautiful young woman. When she was a girl, I wanted to instill a biblical and powerful identity in her. When I talked to her about writing this book, I asked, "Do you remember what I said to you every day as you got out of the car to go to school?"

She instantly smiled and said, "Yes, every day you told me, 'Alex, remember who you are.'"

It's a simple statement with the potential to shape the future . . . for Alex as she attended grade school, and for each of us as we navigate the rough waters of our lives.

We may think our situations are completely hopeless, and consequently, we feel totally helpless. Daniel and Paul (and countless other brave, wise believers over the centuries) show us that's never the case. No matter how depressing our situations may be, we can always fall back into the sovereign, wise, loving arms of almighty God.

Viktor Frankl was a Jewish psychiatrist who was imprisoned in a Nazi concentration camp, and the Germans killed others in his family. Every day, he watched others in the camp. Many had false hopes of early release, and they were devastated when their eager expectations were crushed by harsh realities. In *Man's Search for Meaning*, an account of his insights about human nature in the camps, Frankl explains, "Everything can be taken from a man but one thing: the last of the human freedoms—to choose one's attitude in any given set of circumstances, to choose one's own way."[7]

NOT ALONE

If you feel like the American culture is shifting under your feet and you're powerless to stop it, you're not alone. Many of us see the same powerful undercurrents of history taking place in front of our eyes.

Some people have drifted with the culture and need to remember who they are, returning to their identity and purpose. Others are hanging on by their fingernails to God's will and ways. They need to remember that God will never leave them or forsake them. Yes, the culture is drifting, but God's presence, truth, grace, and power haven't changed at all. He is just as real, just as strong, and just as loving as ever.

When pastors, politicians, or any of us waver because we're afraid, we compromise the truth. But truth isn't flexible. Truth doesn't accommodate. Truth is truth. Whether we've drifted into discouragement or are trying desperately to remain strong in our faith, all of us need to stay focused on God's direction for our lives. He is the "true north," and he will guide us.

As we hold fast to God and his purposes, we won't quietly accommodate the destructive currents of our culture, we won't react in anger to oppose people who disagree with us, and we won't withdraw out of hopelessness and despair. Instead, we'll trust in the matchless love, wisdom, and strength of God to engage the people and causes around us, and we'll shine in the darkness.

At the end of each chapter, I will ask you to remember something about the nature of God and his purposes for you. You'll also find a few questions to help you reflect on the points in the chapter, a prayer, and some passages of Scripture for additional reading. Many small groups and classes will use this book, so they can use the questions as discussion starters. If you have time, go deeper into the passages of Scripture that explain more of our identity, God's purposes, and how you can stay the course.

THINK ABOUT IT . . .
Remember *who* you are and *whose* you are.

1. What are the changes in our culture that are most alarming to you?

2. What might be the motives and hopes when people accommodate the changes in culture, when they fiercely oppose it, when they withdraw, and when they engage with truth and grace?

3. How are Daniel and Paul good examples of how to live for God in a drifting or pagan culture? What traits do they model for us?

Father, fill me with your grace and truth so I can engage my culture instead of drifting with it, being lost in anger and resentment, or giving up in hopelessness.

GO DEEPER . . .

1. What does 1 Pet. 2:9-10 say about your identity in Christ?

2. How does Acts 20:22-24 describe God's purpose for you?

3. How does 2 Cor. 4:7-18 show you how to stand strong and stay on track?

CHAPTER 2

ESTABLISHING TRUE NORTH

You were made by God and for God
and until you understand that,
life will never make sense.

—RICK WARREN

If you pay attention to the ads on television or in magazines, walk down the halls of schools, or listen in on conversations at the office or in church lobbies, you'll hear what matters most to people. Most people tend to be amazed at others who are smart, who have corporate, political, or popular power, and who have more money than anyone else. And more than amazement, if you listen very closely, you'll probably detect a sense of envy. People think they simply can't be happy unless they have as much beauty, power, and wealth as those they've put on a pedestal.

These pursuits are a burning passion for countless people, fed by the fuel of comparison. But like a fire that needs more fuel as it spreads, the thirst for more is never satisfied. In the quest, people become self-absorbed and compete with others, even their best friends. Comparison kills. It ruins relationships, consumes time and energy, and poisons hearts.

In *Mere Christianity*, C.S. Lewis explains that pride is at the heart of comparison:

> Pride gets no pleasure out of having something, only out of having more of it than the next man. We say that people are proud of being rich, or clever, or good-looking, but they are not. They are proud of being richer, or cleverer, or better looking than others. If every one else became equally rich, or clever, or good-looking there would be nothing to be proud about. It is the comparison that makes you proud: the pleasure of being above the rest. Once the element of competition is gone, pride is gone.[8]

THE RIGHT HEADING

There's nothing inherently wrong with wanting to be smart, powerful, or rich, but when those pursuits become the most important things in our lives, they lead us off course. We need God to give us the right heading, a true north.

Throughout history we see that human nature tends to value secondary things as ultimate things. During one of the darkest times in Israel's history, when exile created heartache and famine caused devastation, the Lord spoke through the prophet Jeremiah:

> This is what the LORD says:
> "Let not the wise boast of their wisdom
>   or the strong boast of their strength
>   or the rich boast of their riches,

but let the one who boasts boast about this:
>   that they have the understanding to know me,
> that I am the Lord, who exercises kindness,
>   justice and righteousness on earth,
>   for in these I delight," declares the LORD.
>   (Jer. 9:23-24)

In the ancient world, military leaders "boasted" of their army's strength and courage in the face of an attack. The commander might yell, "Today our army will destroy the enemy and take all their land!" Or, "Our swords are sharper and our arms are stronger. We'll surely win today!" (Think of William Wallace in front of his troops in *Braveheart*.) A "boast" was the commander's declaration of the army's source of strength and their hope of success.

God was saying to Israel—and he's saying to us today—that it's human nature to boast in our intelligence, our power over others, and our bank account and possessions. When we boast in them, it shows that we trust such tangible, temporal things to be our ultimate security and the source of our deepest fulfillment.

History . . . and our families and friendships . . . are littered with evidence that the pursuit of these things gives only temporary joy. Inevitably, our misguided passions produce broken hearts and strained relationships. In our emptiness and desperation, we use people instead of loving them. God's plan is that we worship God, love people, and use things. When our priorities become perverted, we ignore God, love things, and use people. We may use them as pawns in our game to succeed, or we may try to impress them because we can't live without their approval. Either way, we don't really care about those people; we only care that they reinforce our fragile sense of identity.

Ironically, even when you win at this game, you lose. As you climb over people to gain power and prestige, you become more isolated and less lovable. Or when you win approval from others, it creates an insatiable thirst for the next smile, the next pat on the back, the next accolade. Every moment of comparison and every attempt to win approval make you more fragile and empty.

God said there is only one good reason to boast: in response to the wonder of his love so that our hearts are thrilled to know him. The more we truly know God, the more our hearts will delight in the things that give him pleasure: kindness, justice, and righteousness. We'll be amazed that God, the king who lives in unimaginable splendor and majesty, stepped out of heaven to become one of us, loved us enough to pay the price to forgive us, and brought us into his own family. We are "in Christ": identified with him in his death, burial, resurrection, and as he is seated at the right hand of the Father. And all of this is a gift. We didn't earn it; we *couldn't* earn it. A deep sense of gratitude for the grace of God fills our empty hearts to overflowing. Because of God's grace, we have infinite love and ultimate security, so we have no reason to compare ourselves to anyone.

Some of us live a Christian life as if we're always under the stern, watchful eye of our Father and he is very impossible to please. . . . No, God delights even in our heartfelt attempts at obedience.

—Kevin DeYoung

In Christ, we have the source of all wisdom and truth. In him, we have the Spirit's awesome power. And in Jesus, we're wealthy in the things that matter most. We may not understand the chaos that's going on around us, but we're confident that God knows, God cares, and God will give us wisdom to respond in a way that honors him.

Paul occasionally acknowledged his past prestige and accomplishments, but he understood that his credentials no longer mattered. He had been in *Who's Who* of Jewish culture, with the right family connections, an impressive résumé, and plenty of accomplishments. He had boasted in all these things . . . until Christ gave him a very different true north. In his letter to the Philippians, Paul explained that he had come to a conclusion about what's most important:

> But whatever were gains to me I now consider loss for the sake of Christ. What is more, I consider everything a loss because of the surpassing worth of knowing Christ Jesus my Lord, for whose sake I have lost all things. I consider them garbage, that I may gain Christ and be found in him, not having a righteousness of my own that comes from the law, but that which is through faith in Christ—the righteousness that comes from God on the basis of faith. (Phil. 3:7-9)

Paul didn't say Christ and his previous credentials were neck-and-neck in competition for his heart. He said one has ultimate value, and the other is "garbage." To Paul, anything that gets in the way of "the surpassing worth of knowing Christ Jesus" is less than worthless—it's a stinking, rotting mess!

Have you and I come to the same conclusion? Can we say that the things the world values supremely—popularity, position, power, and possessions—are so unimportant that we equate them with the stuff in our trashcans? The only way we can let go of the pursuits the world values is to value something (or someone) far more.

We were made for God, to delight in him above all else, to experience the wonder of his love and to love him in return, and to be his ambassadors in all we say and do. Saint Augustine famously wrote, "You have made us for yourself, O Lord, and our heart is restless until it rests in you."[9] Without having God in the center of our hearts, we wander, we drift, and we're never truly satisfied. But when we invite him to fill our hearts, we experience the rare blend of contentment and zeal, peace and drive. No other pursuit ultimately satisfies. No other heading gives us the right direction. No other life is worth living.

A COMPASS OR A MAP?

Many politicians, business leaders, and pastors are trying to provide a roadmap for people to follow. Maps are helpful, but they soon go out of date. Most of us have had the frustrating experience of following the directions on our phone's GPS when the very sweet and confident voice tells us to take an exit that no longer exists. If we follow directions blindly, we may end up behind an abandoned warehouse, in a cornfield, or stuck on the side of the interstate highway. Maps can be useful, but they aren't foolproof.

A compass, on the other hand, always points due north. No matter where you are or where you've been, the needle shows you magnetic north at that moment. It's the single point of reference you can always rely on. It's unchanging and uncompromising. We may not like the way it points, and we may try to argue with it, but it doesn't change.

Another difference between a compass and a map is that a map almost always offers many routes to get to the same destination. I can ask my phone app for alternate routes so I can pick the one I like. A compass doesn't give alternate directions to magnetic north; it's constant and immovable.

People in today's world are open to many different routes to find God. They may try Buddhism for a while, then Islam or Hinduism, and maybe they'll go to church and check Jesus out. They believe all religions lead to the same place, so one is just as good as another. For such people, being "spiritual" is enough.

Even within Christianity, believers can be unsure about their paths. They hear about some churches that are caring for refugees, but they hear other Christian leaders anxiously describe the threat that some refugees might be terrorists, and they insist on keeping them out of our country. The topic might be guns, abortion, same-sex marriage, healthcare, income distribution, or any of dozens of other issues. Every leader has a map to follow, but too few of the maps point people to the true north where they discover the grace and truth of Jesus Christ.

Even in the church, many people look for a map to happiness and fulfillment, but the routes they take are no different from the paths everyone else in our culture is taking. They try to get a little more knowledge, a little more power and prestige, and a little more money (or a lot more!) in the hope of filling the hole in their hearts. Counterfeit treasures can't satisfy us; they won't, and they never will.

Our spiritual compass always points to Jesus Christ, and it leads us to our identity and our purpose found only in him. David understood the single goal of knowing and loving God. He was the king of Israel, a skilled warrior, and a great leader. As the nation's king, he faced difficult challenges every day. It would have been easy for him to be distracted and overwhelmed, but he kept his eye on the compass. He wrote:

> One thing I ask from the Lord,
>   this only do I seek:
> that I may dwell in the house of the Lord
>   all the days of my life,
> to gaze on the beauty of the Lord
>   and to seek him in his temple. (Ps. 27:4)

David had *one* prayer, *one* desire, and *one* pursuit: to be amazed at the beauty of God's love and power so that God filled his heart. I have to ask myself: Is the beauty of God my one prayer, my one desire, and my one pursuit? Is it yours?

CROSSROADS

In the opening book of the Bible, we read a fascinating story of Isaac's two sons, Esau and Jacob. On first glance, we might conclude that Esau would be the obvious choice for God to use for his purposes. He's the elder brother, he's big and strong, and he works hard. Jacob is lazy, he's a mama's boy, and he has a bad habit of not telling the truth. (In fact, his name means "deceiver.") In ancient times, the law of primogeniture gave the older son a larger share of inheritance to carry on the family name, but Jacob tricked Esau out of his rightful inheritance. Then later, with his mother's help, Jacob deceived his aging father in order to receive the blessing reserved for the elder son.

When they realized what Jacob had done, Isaac was crushed and Esau was enraged! Jacob had to run for his life. His mother told him to go to her homeland to work for her brother Laban. Jacob left his family, his homeland, and his secure position in a prosperous family. Because he chose the road of deception, he lost his identity and his purpose.

In his uncle Laban's home, Jacob had to do something he had never done before: he worked hard. He was motivated by love. He fell head over heels for Rachel, Laban's younger daughter, and he agreed to work seven years as the payment to marry her. This was an exorbitant dowry, far more than the normal amount paid by a suitor for a bride, but Jacob was blinded by passion.

On his wedding day, wine was flowing freely. The bride wore a thick veil, and she followed her drunken husband into the wedding tent that night. The next morning, Jacob woke up and found Rachel's sister Leah lying next to him! Laban had deceived the deceiver. When Jacob confronted him, Laban said that it was never his intention—or his clear commitment—to let his beautiful younger daughter marry before his not-so-beautiful older daughter wed. Laban cut a new deal: he agreed to let Jacob work another seven years for Rachel.

After fourteen years under Laban, Jacob had two competitive wives, eleven sons, and a large herd of livestock. Laban had become suspicious of him, so Jacob decided to return home. On the way, he had second thoughts. What if Esau was still angry? What if he still wanted to kill him? As he approached his homeland, Jacob sent his wives, children, and livestock ahead while he remained alone on the other side of the river Jabbok. Everything he valued was at risk . . . everything might be lost.

> **You never know how much you really believe anything until its truth or falsehood becomes a matter of life and death to you.**
>
> —C.S. LEWIS

The river's name, *Jabbok*, means "emptying." It was an appropriate message that Jacob, a man who had previously been a little too full of himself, needed to acknowledge and embrace. That night an angel of the Lord met with Jacob, and the two of them wrestled all night. As morning broke, Jacob seemed to get the better of the divine visitor, but the angel touched Jacob on the hip, putting it out of joint.

At the crossroads of his life, Jacob met God. The deceiver had an encounter with the truth—the truth about God, the truth about himself, and the truth about his situation. He had to face the facts about his sin and deception, his insecurity and fears. The process of emptying himself was excruciating, and in the end, he limped away with a physical, constant reminder of his dependence on God. God also gave Jacob a new identity and a new name, *Israel*, which means "may God prevail" or "he struggles with God."

At the crossroads near the Jabbok, Jacob took a new road, the road of renewal. Like all of us, the change wasn't instantaneous or complete, but it was a good beginning. Jacob became more truthful, less deceptive, and he lived with more honor than before. Success, pleasure, and power had been the path Jacob had traveled to find meaning in life, but those had brought only personal pain and relational tension. Now he had a new compass reading, a true north of knowing and following God. He could be content, no matter who was upset with him or how his fortunes turned out. But the change had come at a price. Jacob had to become empty before he could be filled, and emptying ourselves is always painful. The old desires and habits have to be pulled out by the roots so they can be replaced by the warmth, forgiveness, and quiet strength of God.

If we peel back a layer or two, we realize Jacob became a deceiver because he was first deceived. He believed he needed to trick his brother to get good things from God, and he (and his mother) thought they must manipulate his father to get God's blessing.

When we don't trust God, we too are deceived. We believe we need to go along with the changes in the culture to be cool, or we assume it's completely up to us to stop the change, or we give up and walk away from meaningful engagement with difficult people and issues. Unbelief and cowardice are signs that we just don't get it! God is still in control.

Daniel and Paul realized they could trust God and serve him even in the worst of cultural oppression. Jacob realized he could experience God and his blessings only when he gave up on orchestrating his life. Trust in God doesn't mean, and it has never meant, passive acceptance. God has called us to stand strong, but always with gentleness, love, and humility.

Sooner or later, all of us come to a crossroads. We may have gone to church for years, or we may be new to the faith, but God brings us to our own Jabbok River where we have to admit our emptiness, the way we've been deceived, and the ways we've tried to deceive others to get what we want from them. In those crucial turning points, we have a choice: to wrestle with God until he touches us with a permanent reminder of his presence, purpose, and power, or turn around and go back to our manipulative habits.

When we submit, acknowledging our emptiness and being filled with God, he gives us a new name. We are no longer "driven," "anxious," "fragile," or "demanding." We are "loved," "forgiven," "accepted," and "the delight of God's heart." With that sense of security, we can move toward the most fearful people, the most demanding situations, and the most difficult problems of our day, and our words and actions are fueled by God's loving presence, awesome power, and kingdom purposes.

Two people can sit side by side at church every week, but with vastly different perspectives on God, culture, and themselves. One reads the Bible through the lens of fear, self-righteousness, and self-pity, and he demands that God, politicians, and church leaders make his life better. The other sees the same problems, but views them through the lens of God's greatness, grace, and wisdom. The first person is full of fear and anger; the second is full of trust and a desire to represent God to anyone who will listen.

MY TRUE NORTH

I grew up in poverty in Humboldt Park in Chicago. My father left home when I was a young boy, leaving my mother to find work to provide for my brothers and me. Two of my older brothers soon joined local gangs, which gave them a different kind of life. I knew my mother was worried about my brothers, and I wanted to support her in every possible way. We stayed in an apartment until my mother couldn't pay the rent. To stay off the streets, we often lived with other family members. I attended five different elementary schools. I was often alone, and I wandered the neighborhoods like the children of Israel in the desert. Poverty, crime, gangs, and police crackdowns were the background noise of my life.

When I was twelve, the Hispanic community in our neighborhood rioted against the Chicago police for three days. Gangs unleashed their fury, throwing rocks, overturning paddy wagons, and looting stores. By the third day, the governor called in the National Guard to restore order. When the riots stopped, the only things remaining were broken glass, burned cars, and pervasive bitterness. I didn't know what was to become of us. I felt vulnerable, helpless, and hopeless.

Two years later, Mayor Daley instituted a summer youth program to involve kids in cleaning up the city. I wanted to participate, so I followed directions to the location in our neighborhood: an Assemblies of God church. When I arrived each morning for work, I noticed a group of kids praying at the altar. My family wasn't religious, and I was surprised that people would pray on a day that wasn't Sunday. To them, prayer didn't appear to be boring. They prayed with deep emotion, they raised their hands, and after they finished, they hugged each other.

I was obviously an outsider and didn't belong to their prayer group, but they treated me like an insider. After a few days, the program supervisor noticed that I was looking intently at those kids each morning. He walked over to me and asked, "Do you know Jesus?"

I answered, "No."

He asked, "Would you like to meet him?"

"Yes," I told him. "Where is he?"

He asked the other kids to gather around me, which scared me. In Humboldt Park, gangs put new members in the middle of a circle for initiations, and they were beaten as a rite of admission. As the kids reached out to put their hands on me and pray, I kept my eyes open to look for flying fists.

Yet all they offered was love, and my heart was touched by their kindness. I prayed to accept Jesus as my Savior, and I began a journey to follow him. I couldn't articulate what it all meant, but I was sure I had come to the biggest crossroads of my life. I was no longer disconnected. I finally felt loved, safe, and sure. I wanted to soak up every moment of my new relationship with God and these friends. My thirst for love was profound. I couldn't get enough!

A few months after I trusted Christ, I attended a youth convention sponsored by the church. One night as I knelt at the altar, a woman came up behind me and touched me on the shoulder. She prayed for a while, and then she spoke to me with the authority and voice of God: "I have called you to be a great leader. Stay on my path. I will bless those who bless you, and I will curse those who curse you."

I was new to the faith, so I didn't recognize that the last sentence was God's promise to Abraham. In fact, I was more amused than impressed by what she said to me. I turned and smiled at her, and she walked away.

A few minutes later, I got into an elevator to go to my room in the hotel. Just before the doors closed, a tall Anglo man stepped in. As we started to go up, he looked intently at me and said, "Have you not heard? I have called you to be a great leader. Stay on my path. I will bless those who bless you, and I will curse those who curse you."

I couldn't wait for the doors to open so I could run away from this guy! I didn't realize it at the time, but God was speaking through those two people to establish the true north in my life. The seed was planted, and I was marked for life. As the meaning of their words gradually sank into my mind and heart, God's clear calling determined my responses to all kinds of situations. When I was in high school and was tempted to do something stupid, I remembered those words and told myself, *Hey, you're going to be a leader. Stop playing around. You have a calling from God. Do the right thing!*

For more than three decades, I've continually gone back to those moments when God spoke to me at the altar and in the elevator. I had been wandering and empty, but God met me to give me a new name, "leader," and a new purpose, to represent him in every moment and in powerful ways.

I have a great need for Christ; I have a great Christ for my need.

—CHARLES SPURGEON

God's clear calling to you may not have come as dramatically, but if you're a Christian, you've heard him call your name. Because we are "in Christ," the Father's words to Jesus at his baptism are his words to you and me. A voice from heaven announced, "This is my Son, whom I love; with him I am well pleased" (Matt. 3:17). Have you heard God speak those words to you? The Father loves you as much as he loves Jesus. And he has a divine purpose for you: to let the life of Jesus shine through you. Amazing!

God may speak to us in any number of ways. We may read a passage of Scripture, and at a particular moment the Spirit of God assures us that we belong to God and he has a specific design for our lives. God's message of unfailing love may be imparted by a parent, an aunt or uncle, a pastor, a spouse, or a friend. God may speak to us in a worship song or in the quiet of our hearts when we're alone in prayer.

As a loving, attentive parent, God's instructions are tailored to each of us. God told the timid Jeremiah to stand up, but he humbled Isaiah with the awesome glory of his presence. The Lord's words may come in very different ways and give very different directions, but we can count on three things: God speaks a message of true north to every child of his; his message is always that we can trust our powerful, loving parent; and he has a specific purpose for us to fulfill. God certainly didn't make his purpose for my life very clear in those early years. It's only in hindsight that I see his hand guiding me to become a leader in our community and in his church.

Through the years, God's voice isn't the only sound I've received. I've heard many competing voices. People have told me, "Choco, you'll never amount to anything. Look at where you've come from," or, "Your teachers don't think you'll make it, so just give up." These poisonous messages don't always come from unbelievers, either. When I was still in high school and trying my best to walk with God, a lady in our church took me aside, pointed her finger at me, and said: "I don't like you." I replied, "I guess we're even because I don't like you either!"

For years, this woman continued to spread gossip to hurt me. When I became a leader in the church, her attacks doubled. And after I got married, she tried to sink her fangs into Elizabeth, too. At every point, I had to remember God's promise to bless those who bless me and curse those who curse me. I didn't want the woman to be harmed, but God's promise assured me that I didn't have to protect myself or lash out in revenge. I could leave justice in God's hands and trust him to take care of her.

Sometimes the voices in our own heads are the hardest to analyze. The enemy of our souls speaks to us in our own voices to question God's motives, his power, and his clear calling. He tempts us to doubt God, just as he tempted Jesus in the desert, but quite often his message sounds completely reasonable because it's formed in our own minds.

God's calling doesn't make us perfect, and it doesn't make us invulnerable to doubts and attacks. But God's calling to a true north of identity and purpose is the constant benchmark that we can go back to again and again when we feel shaken, when we're confused, or when others attack us.

Many times in my life I've had to go back to those precious moments at the altar and the elevator to remember that God has permanently written my name on the palms of his hand, and that has called me to his eternal purpose. God's message of love and purpose has been, and will continue to be, a repeating chorus of hope in my life.

Have you heard God call your name? Has he given you a true north of identity and purpose? Do you need to remember what he has said before, or do you need to hear it for the first time?

Listen. He's speaking.

THINK ABOUT IT . . .

Remember that God has called you to be his dearly beloved child, and he has called you for a kingdom purpose.

1. What are some ads that promise happiness, popularity, and fulfillment? What do they really promise? Why are these ads so effective?

2. In what way is knowing Christ a surpassing value to you? What about him is so marvelous and beautiful?

3. Have you had a river Jabbok experience with God? If so, describe it. If not, what difference would it make?

Father, you have called my name, and you've called me to represent you to the people around me. Thank you that you never leave me or forsake me.

GO DEEPER . . .

1. What does Isa. 49:15-16 say about your identity in Christ?

2. How does Phil. 2:12-16 describe God's purpose for you?

3. How does Phil. 3:12-21 show you how to stand strong and
   stay on track?

CHAPTER 3

STAY ON TRACK

*Our greatest fear should not be of failure,
but of succeeding at things in life
that don't really matter.*

—FRANCIS CHAN

The Russian cruise ship *Lyubov Orlova* was launched in 1976 to explore the Antarctic waters. It was considered impregnable, with a strong, thick hull to withstand the impact of massive icebergs. The ship was named for a popular film star and was the belle of the southern oceans.

After more than three decades, however, the ship lost its usefulness. When harbor fees went unpaid in Newfoundland, a salvage contractor paid the $250,000 owed. Two years later a Caribbean company bought it and hired Transport Canada to tow the now disgraced *Lyubov Orlova* to their scrapyard in the Dominican Republic.

On the way south in the Atlantic, the towline broke and the ship drifted away. The towing barge lost contact, and Transport Canada was unwilling to spend the money to search for it. They were convinced the currents would take the ship into the vast Atlantic Ocean, far away from Canada and the United States.

Months later, U.S. satellites showed the abandoned ship about 1300 nautical miles off the west coast of Ireland. It was still drifting eastward in the current. After that, the ship disappeared. The Irish government tried to locate the "ghost ship," but the *Lyubov Orlova* never made it into their territorial waters. Still later, two signals were picked up, probably from lifeboats that had fallen into the water, but by then no one cared. Most maritime authorities presume the abandoned ship sank in a violent Atlantic storm, but no one really knows. It simply vanished.[10]

Like this ship, our natural tendency is to break away from God and drift away to pursue our own purposes. A student's mind drifts from the teacher's lecture, a spouse's heart drifts during times of boredom or tension, a driver drifts into the next lane when she's daydreaming, and a believer's heart drifts when he assumes God isn't on his throne any longer.

Drift can begin without our even noticing. An ad, a comment, a thought, or a desire captures our hearts. It may be something negative that hurts us, allowing discouragement to take root, or the distraction could come from a new opportunity, an unexpected success, or a romance that becomes the most important thing in our lives. Sometimes a sudden tragic event—severe illness, death, financial reversal, or a shattered dream—can destroy our confidence in God's plan for our future. Eventually disappointment and self-pity cause us to become self-absorbed instead of holding on to our identity and God's great purpose for us. Before we know it, we're like the *Lyubov Orlova*, adrift in a sea of false hopes and broken dreams.

SINCE TIME BEGAN

Throughout the Scriptures, we find a lot of warnings to avoid drifting away from God. There may be many causes, but God's message is always the same: "Watch out! Don't be deceived! Stay on track!" Let's look at a few common causes of drift and see how each one might apply to us today.

We don't drift in good directions.

—ANDY STANLEY

Dissatisfaction

In the opening chapters of the Bible, we find Adam and Eve living in the perfect environment, with a perfect relationship, in the loving presence of God. But for them, it wasn't enough. Satan tempted Eve to "be like God," and she took the bait. After Adam realized what happened, he joined her. When God confronted him, he blamed Eve and he blamed God. Their decision opened the door to sin for all humankind. As a consequence, we are still easily tempted to feel dissatisfied with God and his provisions for us.

Short memories

God miraculously freed the children of Israel from slavery in Egypt, and he opened the Red Sea to let them escape Pharaoh's army. In the desert, he provided water from a rock and manna and quail from the sky. The people, though, forgot all God had done for them, and they began to complain: "The riffraff among the people had a craving and soon they had the People of Israel whining, 'Why can't we have meat? We ate fish in Egypt—and got it free!—to say nothing of the cucumbers and melons, the leeks and onions and garlic. But nothing tastes good out here; all we get is manna, manna, manna'" (Num. 11:4-6, MSG). They must have forgotten that the reason they got free fish is they had been cruelly treated as slaves!

In the same way, we can easily focus on the problems and disappointments of today and forget all God has done for us in the past. A short memory produces a weak faith.

Desire for a better master

Most of us long for a master who will take care of us, but not one who holds us accountable. We want a savior who can do things for us, not one who expects to be obeyed. We want a service provider, not a sovereign King! When God didn't come through for the people during the time of Jeremiah, they quickly turned to other sources to provide excitement and security. The prophet compared the desire for a better master to a camel in heat:

> Well, look at the tracks you've left behind in the valley.
>> How do you account for what is written in the desert dust—
> Tracks of a camel in heat, running this way and that,
>> tracks of a wild donkey in rut,
> Sniffing the wind for the slightest scent of sex.
>> Who could possibly corral her! (Jer. 2:23-24, MSG)

Some might read this and shake their heads, "Really? He's comparing us with a camel in heat? Come on!"

Yes, if we dig down into our hearts, we'll find our deepest and truest motivations. If we thirst for money, we'll daydream about winning the Powerball and spending a fortune on ourselves. If we long for power, we'll daydream about rising to the top positions or winning awards and receiving accolades. If we desire love, we'll daydream about intimate romance or sexual ecstasy. What we think about in our downtime reveals the true condition of our hearts—and it shows us what we value more than anything in the world.

Religious activity without love

Paradoxically, one of the easiest ways to get off track is to be involved in religious activities, but with wrong motives: to show how great we are instead of serving to honor God and care for others. In the gospels, we find Jesus often confronting a group of people who fit this description, the Pharisees. Jesus demonstrated God's love for the unlovely, but the Pharisees saw his compassion as moral compromise. Jesus pleaded with them to embrace God's kindness, but they hated him for looking weak. Finally, he pulled out the big guns and pronounced a series of statements that condemned their narrow, self-righteous, arrogant behavior (Matt. 23:13-38). He told them that, like a tomb, they were clean and white on the outside but their insides were stinking and rotten. And he called them snakes—which meant they were more like Satan than like God. Not surprisingly, they were upset! After all, they were doing all the right religious activities (or so they thought). Jesus' accusations were accurate, but his goal wasn't to condemn. He wanted to expose their hypocrisy so they'd turn back to God and experience his forgiveness and love. Instead, they killed him.

It's amazing that some people can sit in church week after week (and even read their Bibles every day) and still miss Jesus' heart. Instead of experiencing his love and then overflowing with love toward others, some of us stand back and actually criticize those who reach out to care for others.

Distractions

Sometimes people can get so busy doing things for God that they fail to connect with his heart. That was Martha's problem. Mary and Martha were sisters of Lazarus, and all three were Jesus' friends. Once when Jesus stopped at their house for dinner, Mary spent time listening to Jesus while Martha worked in the kitchen. Martha was furious that her sister wasn't helping, so she went to the top: she complained to Jesus! She whined, "Lord, don't you care that my sister has left me to do the work by myself? Tell her to help me!"

Jesus replied, "Martha, Martha, you are worried and upset about many things, but few things are needed—or indeed only one. Mary has chosen what is better, and it will not be taken away from her" (Luke 10:40-42).

Some of us are more like Martha than Mary. We are so busy working to serve God that we miss the one thing he wants to share with us. He offers a genuine, life-changing relationship if we will only stop to spend time with him.

Deception

One way to read Paul's letters is to realize they are constant reminders to avoid drift. He realized three forces pull people away from God: the natural tendency of the human heart to be its own master, the lure of culture and its treasures, and the lies of the enemy. He used harsh terms in his correspondence with the believers in Corinth. He had to! The church was full of bitterness, factions, sexual sin, and false teaching—like many of our churches today. In his second letter, he confides that he is afraid for them. This is pretty amazing because the Apostle Paul never seemed to be afraid of anything! He faced shipwreck, beatings, prison, ridicule, hunger, thirst, and death for the sake of the gospel, so we need to pay attention when he says he's afraid. He wrote, "But I am afraid that just as Eve was deceived by the serpent's cunning, your minds may somehow be led astray from your sincere and pure devotion to Christ" (2 Cor. 11:3).

The enemy still lies to us like he lied to Eve in the Garden. He tries to lure our hearts away from God, and he will use anything and everything to tempt us: success and failure, births and deaths, health and sickness, good friends and fierce enemies, wealth and poverty. At any moment we might hear the whisper, "You don't need God any more," or "You can't trust God any more."

A scared world needs a fearless church.

—A.W. TOZER

Opposition

The Christians in the first century suffered far more persecution than we experience in America today, though believers in other parts of the world still endure horrific abuse. Some of us are fragile, and even a little opposition crushes our spirits. The writer to the Hebrews tried to put steel in the souls of his readers. They were being threatened by both Jews who had rejected Christ and Roman authorities who resisted the new faith that was sweeping the empire. The writer repeatedly encouraged them:

- We must pay the most careful attention, therefore, to what we have heard, so that we do not drift away. For since the message spoken through angels was binding, and every violation and disobedience received its just punishment, how shall we escape if we ignore so great a salvation? (Heb. 2:1-3)

- You suffered along with those in prison and joyfully accepted the confiscation of your property, because you knew that you yourselves had better and lasting possessions. So do not throw away your confidence; it will be richly rewarded. (Heb. 10:34-35)

- Therefore, since we are surrounded by such a great cloud of witnesses, let us throw off everything that hinders and the sin that so easily entangles. And let us run with perseverance the race marked out for us, fixing our eyes on Jesus, the pioneer and perfecter of faith. For the joy set before him he endured the cross, scorning its shame, and sat down at the right hand of the throne of God. Consider him who endured such opposition from sinners, so that you will not grow weary and lose heart. (Heb. 12:1-3)

When we suffer for our faith, we need to fix our eyes on Jesus, who suffered rejection, torture, and death so that we could enjoy acceptance, blessings, and eternal life as a gift from the hand of God.

THE PATTERN OF FAITH

When we look at the faithful people in the Scriptures as well as the individuals of strong faith around us, we notice a distinct pattern: faith, obedience, and blessing. They recognize the power and the goodness of God, take a step of faith in obedience to his command, and sooner or later they enjoy the blessings God pours out on them. This pattern may take years to complete, but God's promises are sure.

In many cases, God's directions may seem odd to us. When a local Christian school found themselves in trouble, they asked me to step in to be the principal. I'm not trained as an educator and I have no experience teaching in schools, but I sensed God's leading in that situation. It was hard and thankless work, but it gave me a voice in the community.

Similarly, I had an opportunity to be on the Zoning Board of Appeals for the city of Chicago. Many people close to me wondered if the responsibilities would distract me from God's calling. Instead, I believed this opportunity was a *vital part* of God's calling, one I hoped would open doors for our church. I got to know many of the leaders in the city, and eventually I was asked to become the Executive Assistant to the CEO of Chicago Public Schools. People often wonder how I know so many leaders in our city. If you know my history, it's not hard to understand. I've served the public in several different roles, and through them all, I've gotten to know the powerbrokers that are involved.

My circle of acquaintances has grown larger each time I've stepped out in faith and obeyed the Lord. I've met leaders of cities, including the mayor of the great city of Chicago. I even got to meet President Barack Obama during a religious gathering. I was grateful for the opportunity, but I didn't imagine the blessings that would follow. God opened doors so that a kid who had grown up feeling lost and alone, with no future and a family moving from place to place, was able to meet the President and even get a personal tour of the White House. Imagine that! Many people don't know this, but we had the privilege of bowling in the White House—just my wife, my kids, and me. In the midst of all of the activity that surrounds our lives, memories like those put a smile on our faces and appreciation in our hearts for a God who gives his children simple pleasures. Sometimes blessings come in unexpected ways.

We seldom (if ever) know the outcome when we answer God's call to obey him. God told Moses to go back to Egypt and tell Pharaoh, "Let my people go," but he had no idea how all that would work out. God didn't tell him that Pharaoh would say "no" and make life even more difficult for the Israelites, and God didn't explain that it would take the miracle of ten devastating plagues to change Pharaoh's mind. Even after the people were freed, they faced what appeared to be certain death at the shores of the Red Sea before God dried the seabed to allow the people to escape. And God didn't give Moses any indication that it would take an extra forty years to lead a stubborn, complaining group of knuckleheads before they got to their new homeland.

When God called Abraham to leave Ur, he only told him, "Go from your country, your people and your father's household to the land I will show you" (Gen. 12:1). God promised to make the old man and his wife "a great nation" and protect them along the way, but God didn't whisper the rest of the story—that Abraham and Sarah would have to wait twenty-five long years for their son to be born. God promised to create a great nation for Abraham's descendents, but the only land

Abraham and his wife ever possessed was their graves. The great man trusted in the promises of God, and he obeyed, but the fulfillment of blessings took quite a while.

God's path is often revealed one step at a time, so we need strong faith in God's character even when we don't fully grasp his leading. (If he showed us the whole picture, many of us might not take the first step.) As we respond in obedience, God confirms his calling and increases our faith, sometimes through obvious blessings and answers to prayer, but other times in spite of the absence of blessings and the frustrating delays in answering our prayers. Our faith isn't in the outcome; our faith is in the one who calls us.

As a young believer, I was worried that I might miss the will of God, but as I've grown in my faith, I've realized it's not important for me to know every detail before I take a step. The important thing is to trust God and obey immediately when I hear his voice. I don't demand guarantees, and I don't expect an easy path.

When I talk to Christians, many of them want to know the end before they're willing to take the first (or next) step with God. We can be sure he will lead, but we can also be sure it will be an adventure. God will open the next door only after we've walked through the previous one. Moses, Abraham, Paul, and of course, Jesus, show us that following God inevitably leads to greater tests than we ever expected and greater blessings than we ever imagined. Abraham had no idea how God would multiply his descendents to be more numerous than the stars in the sky and the sand on the seashore, but he took the steps God asked him to take.

Many people mistakenly believe following God means he will open every door and make our paths smooth and pleasant.

These people haven't looked very closely at the life of Jesus! He fully obeyed the Father, and his complete faithfulness led him into wonderful moments of miracles and changed lives, but also to rejection, suffering, and death. Not long ago, I met with a minister who was ready to quit the ministry. When I asked him what brought him to this decision, he told me, "I feel God is leading me in a different direction. It's time for a change." But this wasn't our first conversation about God's path for his life. I reminded him what he had told me just two months before: "Pastor Choco, I want to go into full time ministry." I couldn't believe how quickly he had switched from a commitment to full time ministry to quitting. He admitted he was "tired" and "frustrated" with ministry. Sometimes we claim to be led by God when we're really saying, "This is really hard, and I want to give up!"

To follow God's will, we need wisdom to stay on track. We need to position ourselves so we're ready to say "yes" whenever he gives us a command. This means we live "lean and ready," not overloaded by debt and not having our minds troubled by worries. To hear from God, we have to be listening to God. This means we regularly feed on his Word, spend time in prayer, and share life with mature people who will tell us the truth. Then, like a trained and equipped commando, we're ready to obey our leader's orders. Quite often, the first steps are small ones, but they're important. If we insist on waiting until we have all the answers or hold out for a "big enough" assignment, we'll stay stuck in neutral. We have to take a step into the unknown before God reveals our next step. As we obey, we prove to the Lord, to ourselves, and to everyone who's watching that we're fully God's.

We also need the wisdom to say "no" to distractions. Not all open doors are ones God wants us to walk through. Some of them lead away from God's purposes for us. When an opportunity promises a higher title or a greater income, we need to filter it through the grid of our identity and God's purpose. If it doesn't fit, we need to pursue a different opportunity.

A leader in our state asked me to run for the U.S. Senate from Illinois. It was quite a compliment, but it wasn't in line with what God has called me to be and do for his kingdom. I said, "Thank you for thinking of me. I'm honored, but I'm not the right person for the job. God has given me another purpose."

I've learned to walk through open doors to see what God has for me on the other side. I may not fit a particular role very well—like being a school principal—but each time, stretching experiences teach me to depend on God. I meet people I would never have known, and I develop skills that would have lain dormant. Many of the roles I've played were longer than I would have expected. I was a principal for two years, and I learned a lot during that time. If I'd left sooner, I don't think I would have had nearly the impact, and I wouldn't have gained the perspectives on education that will stick with me for the rest of my life.

HOW CAN WE BE SURE?

People often ask me about God's direction for their lives, and the big question usually is: "Pastor, how can I *be sure* this is what God wants for me?" We can be absolutely certain of some things in our walks with God, but not everything. When we look at the vastness of space, we know God is far more powerful and majestic than our minds can comprehend. When we consider the cross, we realize his love is deeper than the deepest ocean. On these two things, we can stake our lives and our futures.

All the rest, I've learned, is details. To be honest, I don't worry about the will of God any longer because I trust that God will lead, and if I get off track, he has promised to work everything out for good for those who trust him—people like you and me.

I spend my time now preparing myself to hear the voice of God so I can obey as soon as I sense his leading. After Paul explained the wonders of the gospel of grace, he told the believers in Rome:

> Therefore, I urge you, brothers and sisters, in view of God's mercy, to offer your bodies as a living sacrifice, holy and pleasing to God—this is your true and proper worship. Do not conform to the pattern of this world, but be transformed by the renewing of your mind. Then you will be able to test and approve what God's will is— his good, pleasing and perfect will. (Rom. 12:1-2)

This passage is very clear and strong. To help people experience the will of God, Paul is prescriptive:

- Reflect often on God's great mercy. Understanding and experiencing God's grace produces both humility and courage. Because of the cross of Christ, we're loved, forgiven, and accepted, so we have nothing to fear when we face life's challenges and when God calls us to obey.

- Offer yourself to God every moment of every day, holding nothing back, always ready to respond to his invitation and command. We belong to him; this is a truth that comforts us and calls us to respond in faith. A life of service is true worship.

- Recognize the lure of our culture to value success, pleasure, and approval, but refuse to bite. We don't pattern our lives after what the world values. These attractive but poisonous messages confuse us, make us critical, and ruin our relationships. Those negative voices can't be completely shut out because we live "in the world," but we're not "of the world."

- Every day, get in the presence of God to praise him, confess your sins, and ask him for wisdom and provisions. If we hurry through our prayers, we may check off all our requests on the list, but we'll miss the strength and encouragement of being in God's presence.

- And obey. When he calls, answer by taking steps of faith. At every point, continue to listen for him to whisper, "Turn here," "Say this to that person," or "Go there." As we take these steps, the path of God becomes clearer.

Let me give a very recent example of the challenge and joy of obeying God. I had cleared my schedule for a day to work on a chapter of this book. Yet as I began, I felt the Lord lead me to meet with several young pastors in our city. It was one of those thoughts that came "out of the blue." Of course, my mind began to rationalize, "It's too last-minute" and "What if they're too busy?" In spite of those thoughts, I decided to obey immediately. Surprisingly, four of the five pastors I invited to lunch that day were able to make it. As soon as we sat down to meet, one of them said, "Thank you. You are an answer to prayer. Just last night my wife and I cried out, 'God, please send us someone to encourage us!' Thank you, Pastor, for your obedience." We spent a raw, refreshing, and encouraging time in each other's company.

On another occasion about a year ago, I picked up the phone to send a text to encourage a fellow pastor. We had met very briefly two years earlier at a major conference and hadn't communicated since then, but the Spirit put him on my heart at that moment. I thought, *I want to write him an encouraging word.* It only took a few minutes of my time . . . a small inconvenience. I wasn't even sure he would remember who I was, but it seemed like the right thing to do. Later he told me he had literally been on his knees at that moment. He was about to quit the ministry, and he was asking God for a sign. He said, "When I got your text, I almost fell over!" Although I didn't really remember him very well, God remembered him, and the Holy Spirit took that moment to stir my heart for this man. I had no idea what he was going through—but God saw him in his moment of need. Since then, we have established a true mentorship relationship. He didn't quit. He's still growing his church, and he's filled with renewed hope for the future. He is a blessing to me and an amazing reminder of how God brings his people together to meet needs when we obey.

When I was a young believer, I worried that I might miss the will of God for my life. This anxiety only led me to doubt that God would speak clearly to me and wonder if my ears were open enough to hear him. I eventually realized all my worries were a waste of time. I now focus my attention on abiding in his Word and expecting him to lead me where he wants me to go. Like every child, sometimes I miss my Father's best—I misunderstand what he's saying or I wait too long to act—but God somehow uses even those detours for good . . . in me and through me to touch the lives of others.

God has given me big dreams to be involved in his work to redeem a lost and broken world, but I didn't start with grand plans. I wasn't exactly "Most Likely to Succeed" in my class. When I was a kid, I just tried to survive each day. I wasn't sure where we were going to live or what school I was going to attend. During my entire childhood through high school graduation I slept on the floor next to a radiator. I didn't sleep in a bed until I moved out on my own. Each tenant shared the kitchen and bathroom—my home was more like a dorm than an apartment. As a kid, my world was full of uncertainty. Life was unsettled. I lived in the moment. I didn't dare to dream of anything beyond making it one more day.

But God had far greater dreams for me than I imagined. I've received accolades and honors that would have been inconceivable to anyone who knew me in those difficult early years. I'm what sociologists call a "status inconsistency." Because of the marvelous grace of God, he "has rescued me from the dominion of darkness and brought [me] into the kingdom of the Son he loves" (Col. 1:13). He saved me from a life of emptiness and gave me a bold, compelling purpose to engage our culture with his grace and truth.

I'm not the only one. God offers the same revolutionary status inconsistency to everyone who will respond and take his hand. If we belong to God, we are citizens of heaven and aliens on earth.

What is God's will for each of us? It's very clear: to respond to his grace and to delight in his presence, power, and purpose . . . to watch for signs of drift so we can make corrections and stay on track . . . to refuse to conform to the world's will and ways, and keep our eyes focused on God . . . to readily confess sin and complacency to God, and to confess to those we've hurt in any way . . . and to devote our lives to kindness, justice, and righteousness on earth, knowing that God delights in these qualities.

> **To live by grace means to acknowledge my whole life story, the light side and the dark. In admitting my shadow side, I learn who I am and what God's grace means.**
>
> —BRENNAN MANNING

Find out what pleases God, and invest your heart in doing those things. In every book of the Bible, we find crystal-clear indications of God's nature and his will. For instance, in Ephesians, Paul uses the metaphor of changing clothes to illustrate the choices of spiritual life. When we realize a shirt or coat is dirty, we don't sit around and hope a clean one will magically appear on our bodies. We intentionally take off the dirty one and put on the clean one. Every moment of every day, we "put off [the] old self, which is being corrupted by its deceitful desires . . . and put on the new self, created to be like God in true righteousness and holiness" (Eph. 4:22-24).

Paul was a practical leader. He didn't want to leave his readers wondering what he was talking about, so he gave them several specific examples: put off lies and speak truth, put off harmful anger and put on righteous anger, stop stealing and work hard so you can be generous, stop using corrosive words and use only those that build people up, get rid of bitterness and put on the kindness, compassion and forgiveness of Christ

(Eph. 4:25-32). I can almost hear Paul asking them, "Is that clear enough for you?"

We don't have to wonder if we're to apply these instructions to our particular situations. They apply to *all* of us *all* the time. It doesn't matter what your spiritual gift may be, and your family background doesn't get you off the hook. These are God's clear directives to all of his children. But Paul doesn't just shake his finger at people and demand, "Try harder!" In a beautiful shift to the *why* behind all the *whats* of God's will, Paul reminds us of Jesus: "Follow God's example, therefore, as dearly loved children and walk in the way of love, just as Christ loved us and gave himself up for us as a fragrant offering and sacrifice to God" (Eph. 5:1-2). Paul continually points to the sacrifice of Christ as our motivation to obey. We obey not out of fear of punishment, but out of a deep desire to please the one who gave himself—completely—for us and to us.

Don't be paralyzed by the fear of missing God's will, and don't put narrow restrictions on how you serve him. Respond to the wonderful love of God and dive in. If you don't fit in a particular role, give it a little time—God may have something to teach you there. In my early years, my pastor asked me to be involved in the children's ministry, and in fact, I was in charge of the puppets. (Yes, puppets.) I was terrible at it, and I completely ruined the puppet ministry for the kids in our church, but I was available and willing. If a room needed painting, I grabbed a bucket and brush. If a truck needed to be unloaded, I showed up. If a class needed a teacher, I studied and gave them my very best. I didn't have any restrictions, and I didn't make any demands.

When you see an opportunity to touch lives, go for it. Some people pray for months before they say "yes" to an opportunity.

For God's sake, pray and then just get to it! Let the love of Jesus fill you and flow through you, and watch what God does in the lives of those you touch. And let's be clear: our service for God isn't always within the walls of the church. We belong to him every minute of every day, and we may have a greater impact in our neighborhoods, shops, businesses, schools, and organizations than we have in the church organizational structure. Support the church, but be open to God using you wherever you go.

The writer to the Hebrews spends his entire letter (actually, a transcribed sermon) encouraging persecuted people to stay on track in following Jesus. He wrote eloquently and often about the sacrifice of Christ for us. In his concluding instructions, he made a connection of two sacrifices we make: "Through Jesus, therefore, let us continually offer to God a sacrifice of praise—the fruit of lips that openly profess his name. And do not forget to do good and to share with others, for with such sacrifices God is pleased" (Heb. 13:15-16).

A heart of praise to God inevitably leads to a life poured out for others. The opposite is true as well: a heart that grumbles and is discontented, critical, and full of doubts about the greatness and grace of God inevitably produces a life that is self-absorbed and narrow.

What's in your heart? Focus on Jesus and stay on track.

THINK ABOUT IT . . .

Remember that faith in God always leads to obedience, which eventually produces God's blessings.

1. What are some ways people are tempted to drift away from "sincere and pure devotion to Christ"? What are the lures? What are some reasons we fall for the deception?

2. How do you see the pattern of faith, obedience, and blessing in your life?

3. We may not be able to see into the future, but we can be absolutely sure of the most important elements of God's will. What are the things we can be sure of?

Lord Jesus, create more of the two sacrifices in me: praise for your greatness and grace . . . and a willingness to serve anytime, anywhere.

GO DEEPER . . .

1. What does Eph. 1:3-14 say about your identity in Christ?

2. How does Rom. 12:1-2 describe God's purpose for you?

3. How does Rom. 5:1-5 show you how to stand strong and stay on track?

CHAPTER 4

KEEP COMING BACK

Any concept of grace that makes us feel
more comfortable sinning is not biblical grace.
God's grace never encourages us to live in sin,
on the contrary, it empowers us to say no to sin
and yes to truth.

—RANDY ALCORN

When an airplane flies from one destination to another, it never
follows a precise route. Winds push the plane left or right, and
columns of air cause it to rise or fall. Tailwinds or headwinds
must be accounted for in order to arrive on time. During the
entire flight, either the human pilot or the autopilot makes con-
tinual corrections.

On a tour of the sleek jet Concorde years ago, a guide
explained the need for instantaneous and constant flight corrections, and a man asked, "Is the plane ever on course?"

"Yes," the guide explained, "about one percent of the time."

A pilot on the New York to Los Angeles flight doesn't wait until the plane is over Seattle before initiating a course change. From the time the plane is in the air, he starts making hundreds, maybe thousands of small changes to keep coming back to the flight plan.

This is a good metaphor for my life, and I suspect it applies to yours as well. We shouldn't be surprised that we drift away from God and his plan for us. Wavering off course is entirely normal for flawed, finite human beings, even those who genuinely want to follow God with all their hearts. We need mid-course corrections . . . lots of them! When we notice the need to come back to God, we take three steps: we admit we've strayed, we thank God for his forgiveness, and we make a new commitment to the flight plan. It's called repentance.

Today, however, repentance has gotten a bad rap. In our culture, we don't want to talk about sin that needs to be forgiven. Instead of "sin," we substitute other terms: "mistakes," "weaknesses," or "bad decisions." People try to avoid responsibility by claiming, "I didn't mean it," "I couldn't help it," or "It's not my fault!"

Heart-suffering because of sin is the best proof that the Holy Spirit dwells in your heart.

—JOHANN ARNDT

To many of us today, the word "sin" is offensive because it implies right and wrong. In a world that puts supreme value on tolerance, we prefer to let people do their own thing "if they think it's right," to "live and let live," and to avoid hurting anyone's feelings. The problem is that the cleansing of God's forgiveness doesn't apply to an innocent mistake. Christ died to save sinners, and he has forgiven the sins committed by Christians. The cross simply doesn't make much sense when we don't acknowledge sin.

When Martin Luther launched the Protestant Reformation by nailing his Ninety-five Theses to the Wittenberg church door in 1517, the first one read: "When our Lord and Master Jesus Christ said, 'Repent' (Matt. 4:17), he willed the entire life of believers to be one of repentance." Luther understood that the Christian life cannot be lived without constant corrections to come back to God and his purposes.

Why, then, does repentance seem so repulsive, or at least out of place, to some believers? Because many of us have a distorted view of sin, and therefore, of the meaning of forgiveness.

A BETTER DEFINITION

When people hear the word "sin," many assume harsh condemnation is only a heartbeat away. They have visions of long, boney fingers pointed at them in anger, or religious fanatics who can't stand the idea of people having any fun. We need a deeper grasp of the meaning of sin. Seminary president and professor Cornelius Plantinga asserts that all of us have an innate sense of right and wrong. It's our God-given conscience. In the core of our souls, we realize evil, chaos, heartache, and injustice were never God's design for us. Instinctively, we know things aren't the way they're supposed to be.

The ancient prophets, Plantinga asserts, foretold of a time when everything will be made right, when justice and righteousness would roll like mighty waters (Amos 5:24). The word God uses to describe his desire for us is *shalom*, which is "the webbing together of God, humans, and all creation in justice, fulfillment, and delight." Shalom includes the concept of peace, but it's far more than that. "In the Bible shalom means universal flourishing, wholeness, and delight. . . . Shalom, in other words, is the way things are supposed to be."[11]

Sin, then, is any violation of shalom, any attack on God's good purposes for any person. Does God hate sin? Yes, but not because he delights in blasting people who sin. God hates sin because it disrupts his beautiful plans for his people.

Does this definition matter? Absolutely! If we redefine sin as only weaknesses and mistakes, we don't see much need for God's cleansing flood. But a superficial understanding of sin doesn't let us off the hook emotionally and spiritually. Instinctively, we know something's wrong. We live with a vague sense of shame that we aren't what we should be, but we have no way to do anything about it.

On the other hand, many Christians define sin narrowly as "breaking God's laws." This concept misses the important truth that sin is actually breaking God's heart because it's a violation of his deep desire for our good, our shalom. If we believe that sin is only breaking God's laws, we try to hide our sins, we rationalize them like they don't matter, or we beat ourselves up because we're sure we deserve punishment. None of those responses are what God has in mind for repentance! When we respond in these ways, we miss the blessing of forgiveness and the refreshment of God's love, and we continue to drift away from God's heart.

What comes into our minds when we think about God is the most important thing about us.

—A.W. TOZER

TWO KINDS OF REPENTANCE

Our definition of sin and our concept of God's grace shape our response when God's Spirit whispers that we need to repent. Paul describes two very different kinds of repentance to the Corinthians. He wrote:

> Even if I caused you sorrow by my letter, I do not regret it. Though I did regret it—I see that my letter hurt you, but only for a little while—yet now I am happy, not because you were made sorry, but because your sorrow led you to repentance. For you became sorrowful as God intended and so were not harmed in any way by us. Godly sorrow brings repentance that leads to salvation and leaves no regret, but worldly sorrow brings death. See what this godly sorrow has produced in you: what earnestness, what eagerness to clear yourselves, what indignation, what alarm, what longing, what concern, what readiness to see justice done. (2 Cor. 7:8-11)

When Paul pointed out sin in the Corinthians' lives in an earlier letter, he wasn't thrilled to condemn them! He loved them, and he longed for them to walk with God. Sin, he knew, hurt them and blocked their experience of God's presence and purpose. He wasn't happy his letter had produced sorrow, but he was very pleased that their sorrow led them to return to God. Paul contrasts "godly sorrow" and "worldly sorrow": one results in life, joy, love, and power, but the other produces a form of emotional and spiritual "death."

Godly sorrow is the gateway to refreshment in the Spirit, a renewed appreciation that God is our loving heavenly Father who wants the best for us. When we grasp this truth, we welcome the Spirit's whisper to repent, and we gladly respond so we can experience the forgiveness Christ has already bought for us. But that's not the end of the benefits. A fresh infusion of forgiveness inspires our hearts, enflames our passions, and propels us to engage with the people around us. This kind of repentance is attractive, powerful, refreshing, and it can happen often in the life of believers. This kind of sorrow doesn't minimize sin—we are fully aware that our sins required the death of the Son of God to pay for them. But it also doesn't minimize grace—Jesus willingly went to the cross because he loves us.

Some people get tripped up when they read that godly sorrow produces repentance "that leads to salvation." They assume Paul is talking only about the moment of conversion when a person initially trusts in Christ. The New Testament points to three tenses of salvation: past, present, and future. We "have been saved" when we trusted in Jesus (Eph. 2:8-9), we are "being saved" as God works his grace into us day by day (1 Cor. 1:18; 2 Cor. 2:15), and someday we will be finally and gloriously saved when we see Jesus face to face (Rom. 5:9; 8:29–30). Paul is saying that repentance is a part—a vital part—of how God transforms us more and more into the image of Jesus as we respond to him in faith. It's the present tense form of salvation.

Worldly sorrow is the opposite of godly sorrow. Instead of bringing refreshment, it crushes our spirits and leaves us with a deep sense of shame. We know we've done wrong, but instead of trusting in God's love and forgiveness, we try to overcome it by feeling bad enough long enough. We know something's terribly wrong with us, but we assume it's up to us to make things right. We hope that our shame will impress God (and maybe others who are watching) so he'll let us off the hook. The problem is that we usually do something else wrong before we've finished paying for the sin, and the shame multiplies. Shame can take many forms: self-hatred, calling ourselves nasty names, withholding joy, withdrawing from pleasures, isolation from others . . . all to punish ourselves for our sins.

Godly sorrow trusts God to cleanse us from sin by the sacrifice Christ has already made for us. It makes us love God more. Worldly sorrow tries to self-justify through penance (activities designed to make up for the sin) or vicious self-blame, which reinforces the shame. It leaves us farther and farther from God's heart. People who experience godly sorrow *love to repent* because it reminds them over and over again of the wonder of the cross. Those who suffer from worldly sorrow *hate to repent* because it reminds them they're defective, deficient, helpless, and hopeless.

When we feel convicted that we've sinned, whether we respond with shame or thankfulness depends on our understanding of God. Many people go to church each week and hear about the grace, power, and wisdom of God, but it doesn't sink in. They see him as a Santa Claus who dispenses blessings, or maybe a senile grandfather who means well but isn't really paying attention. At the other extreme are those who still assume God is a harsh, demanding judge waiting for them to make a mistake so he can blast them!

Stephen Charnock was a Puritan pastor in the mid 1600's. We tend to think of the Puritans as stern and focused primarily on keeping the rules, yet he urged his listeners to think deeply about their perceptions of God. The essence of his teaching was that when we sin, some of us expect God to respond like a provoked, angry lion. But if we believe we belong to a God of kindness and mercy, we realize our sin is like offending a close friend. These opposite concepts of God make a lot of difference! If we see God as furious at us, we'll repent only because we're afraid of what he might do to us. But if we believe God is loving, kind, and generous, we'll repent because we don't want anything to come between us and the one who loves us.[12]

When you sin, do you think of God as a forgetful old man who doesn't even notice, as a ferocious lion who wants to tear you to pieces, or as a dear friend whose feelings you've hurt? Your mental image of God makes a world of difference in how you respond.

THE TRIGGER

Repentance and confession go hand in hand. Repentance means to "turn" or "turn around." The trigger is confession, which means "to agree." When we respond to correction from the teaching of God's Word, the voice of the Spirit, or the warning of a trusted Christian, we agree with God about the sin: "Yes, Lord, what I said or did was wrong." We agree with him about our forgiveness: "Thank you, Lord, that Jesus has already paid for that sin." And we agree with God about the direction we need to take: "Lord, I'm turning from that choice (or habit), and I choose your will and your ways. Give me strength and wisdom to honor you in all I do."

Let's make it clear: confession and repentance don't earn God's forgiveness. God's grace is a free gift offered to all. When we confess and repent, we're not asking God to do something new; we're remembering what he has already done and making it real in our experience. Sin distorts our experience of God's love, forgiveness, acceptance, and direction. But when we agree and turn around, we're tapping into the vast sea of God's love and his good purposes for us. Confession is our handle on forgiveness.

The Apostle John invites us to be ruthlessly honest about our sins because God has given us complete assurance of his forgiveness: "If we claim to be without sin, we deceive ourselves and the truth is not in us. If we confess our sins, he is faithful and just and will forgive us our sins and purify us from all unrighteousness" (1 John 1:8-9). God is glad to forgive his disobedient children. He is "faithful and just" because the penalty for our sin has already been completely paid on the cross. Jesus' last words from the cross were, "It is finished" (John 19:30). The final sacrifice was made, and God's judgment was satisfied.

How do we know if our confession and repentance are "godly sorrow" or "worldly sorrow"? It's easy. Does admitting sin make us feel small and ashamed? Does it make us want to hide from God and lie to those around us? Or does it produce a fresh wave of God's grace that brings us both relief and gratitude? If it's not relief and gratitude, it's not his grace we've found.

The pilot of the airplane doesn't feel shame when he responds to indications the plane has veered slightly off course. He realizes making corrections are good, right, and necessary to stay on track. In the same way, an accurate understanding of godly repentance enables us to experience a little more shalom.

With this kind of repentance, we can keep coming back on track.

True repentance requires humility. All sin is an attempt to take God's place of authority. Like Adam and Eve in the Garden, we want to run our own lives, and we want our will to prevail. When the Spirit shows us we've sinned, the sin has to be exposed and put to death, and deaths are always messy. We'd rather make excuses, blame others, or deny the sin—anything to keep from having to be honest about what happened. In repentance, like every other part of our spiritual lives, real life is possible only through death. We have to let go of our demands, our rights, and our misguided hopes. We let them die so the life of Christ can be renewed in us. That's repentance.

The wonderful news is that our Lord is a God of mercy, and He responds to repentance.

—BILLY GRAHAM

Some have asked, "How often do I need to repent?" or "If I come to the altar on Sunday morning, is that enough?" By all means, come to the altar and pour your heart out to God and receive assurance of his gracious forgiveness, but don't let that be the only time you repent. Remember the airline pilots. I'm glad they don't wait until Sunday morning to make course corrections when I'm flying cross-country during the week! Stay in the Word. As you read it, the Spirit will show you any sinful attitudes or actions and assure you of God's grace. Hebrews tells us:

For the word of God is alive and active. Sharper than any double-edged sword, it penetrates even to dividing soul and spirit, joints and marrow; it judges the thoughts and attitudes of the heart. Nothing in all creation is hidden from God's sight. Everything is uncovered and laid bare before the eyes of him to whom we must give account. . . . Let us then approach God's throne of grace with confidence, so that we may receive mercy and find grace to help us in our time of need. (Heb. 4:12-13, 16)

Others have asked, "Shouldn't I need to repent less as I grow in my faith?" Actually, no. As we grow in our love for God and our sensitivity to the Spirit, we're more open to his voice. We treasure our closeness with God, and we don't want anything to hinder our relationship with him. As we grow, we won't wait as long to confess and repent. We'll be more secure in God's love, so we'll be more willing to admit when we're sinning—even those sins that only we know about.

We're not alone in our struggle. The great Apostle Paul realized and admitted he hadn't arrived (Phil. 3:12-14). In fact, he expected to wrestle with sin for the rest of his life (Rom. 7:14-25).

God has given you incredible resources to help you. Listen to the voice of the Holy Spirit. Trust him to show you what corrections need to happen. And spend time around mature, godly people who are humble and demonstrate a life of repentance.

When I look at the word "repentance," I think of a penthouse, the place of honor and blessing. When we repent, we're returning to that place where we experience the love of God, the strength of God, the presence of God, the joy of God. Get out of the basement of denial, excuses, and shame, and go back to the penthouse. It's the place all of us want to be. In the base-ment, we can only see the interior walls; we feel alone and we can't see out. But when we're in the penthouse, we have a better view . . . and we're amazed. God invites us to enjoy "the extrav-agant dimensions of Christ's love. Reach out and experience the breadth! Test its length! Plumb the depths! Rise to the heights! Live full lives, full in the fullness of God" (Eph. 3:19, MSG).

Why in the world wouldn't we want to go back to the pent-house? It's where we belong. Paradoxically, our willingness to be honest about sin opens the door to more of God's love and forgiveness than ever before. I'm not suggesting sin is good, but God uses it for good if we'll let him.

When I was eighteen, I'd been a Christian for four years. I'd heard many sermons about God's love and forgiveness, and I learned more about the necessity of repentance. One day as I prayed, I asked God, "Is there anything in my life that displeases you? Is there anything that I need to deal with?"

Almost immediately, the Holy Spirit spoke to me, "You're still bitter toward your father for leaving the family." There was no reason to deny it. The resentment in my heart was very real. For years, I'd written my father off. I had concluded that since he didn't want to have anything to do with me, I didn't want to have anything to do with him. My reasons had seemed simple and clear, but suddenly, the logic fell apart. I realized I hated my father for what he had done to us. God was my heavenly Father, and I felt secure in his love. Now it was time to please God by doing what he does to sinners: he forgives them. I prayed, "Lord, show me what you want me to do." The answer came very quickly.

At the time, my father lived in New Jersey. I hadn't seen him since I was a young boy. I asked my mother for his phone number, and I called him. I said, "Dad, this is your son." He was surprised to hear from me. I then said, "I'm calling to tell you that I forgive you. I've resented you leaving us. It's been very hard on my mother, my brothers, and me, but I forgive you."

This conversation opened the door of reconciliation. There were no guarantees my father would walk through that door, and I had no assurances that rebuilding a broken relationship would be easy or quick. But I had opened the door, and gradually, God healed the hurts and gave me a heart of compassion and love for my father.

Our lives begin to end the day we become silent about things that matter.
—MARTIN LUTHER KING, JR.

REPENTANCE AND ENGAGEMENT

The practice of repentance makes a difference in how we engage people in our culture. It's easy for us to ignore people in need and criticize those who hold opposing views. Repentance helps us experience forgiveness and grace in our own lives so that we are able to treat people the way Jesus did in his world. We have to fill the well before we can draw from it: We can love the unlovely only to the extent we've experienced the unconditional love of God: "This is love: not that we loved God, but that he loved us and sent his Son as an atoning sacrifice for our sins. Dear friends, since God so loved us, we also ought to love one another" (1 John 4:10–11). We can forgive those who offend us only to the degree we're amazed that God has forgiven our sins: "Bear with each other and forgive one another if any of you has a grievance against someone. Forgive as the Lord forgave you" (Col. 3:13). And we can accept those who are different from us only as much as we realize that we were outsiders but Christ warmly welcomed us: "Accept one another, then, just as Christ accepted you, in order to bring praise to God" (Rom. 15:7). Our experience of the love, forgiveness, and acceptance of God gives us a blend of boldness and compassion to engage the people around us.

Too many believers have plenty of boldness but not enough compassion. Far too often, Christians who stand up for truth in our culture are harsh and judgmental, completely lacking tenderness, understanding, and kindness. Repentance reminds us who we are—recipients of God's amazing grace—so when we stand up for truth, we never feel superior or communicate in a harsh, judgmental tone. And we listen to those who disagree with us because we realize they are valuable people created in the image of God. The kindness of God has led us to repentance (Rom. 2:4), and the kindness of God flowing through us just might lead others to repentance, too.

IT'S YOUR TURN

God has given us everything we need to walk with him in strength and love, but we live with an inner conflict: we want God's will, but we also crave our own. Paul wrote to a church that was having tremendous struggles with selfishness, fighting, and arrogance. He gave them instruction and an understanding of what's found in the depths of our souls: "So I say, walk by the Spirit, and you will not gratify the desires of the flesh. For the flesh desires what is contrary to the Spirit, and the Spirit what is contrary to the flesh. They are in conflict with each other, so that you are not to do whatever you want" (Gal. 5:16-17).

Professor and theologian D.A. Carson provides some insights about this struggle and our need for constant vigilance:

> People do not drift toward holiness. Apart from grace-driven effort, people do not gravitate toward godliness, prayer, obedience to Scripture, faith, and delight in the Lord. We drift toward compromise and call it tolerance; we drift toward disobedience and call it freedom; we drift toward superstition and call it faith. We cherish the indiscipline of lost self-control and call it relaxation; we slouch toward prayerlessness and delude ourselves into thinking we have escaped legalism; we slide toward godlessness and convince ourselves we have been liberated.[13]

We're in a struggle for our souls, and we have choices every day. It's time to stop making excuses. It's time to make things right—with God and with those around us.

Have you been living in the basement or the penthouse? Take God's hand and rise where he wants you to be. Let me offer a few suggestions:

Evaluate your concept of God.

Have you perceived God as a Santa-Claus-like grandfather who's nice but not very observant? Have you seen him as a policeman looking for someone to catch, or a harsh judge who delights in handing out cruel punishments? Or have you seen him as a loving Father who has high standards, but always wants the very best for you? One of the best indications of your true view of God is how you respond during the moments the Holy Spirit convicts you of sin.

Invite God to shine a light on your heart.

David prayed, "Search me, God, and know my heart; test me and know my anxious thoughts. See if there is any offensive way in me, and lead me in the way everlasting" (Ps. 139:23-24). If we ask God to reveal anything in us that displeases him, he'll show us. Sometimes he may remind us of a recent unkind comment we assumed was no big deal, but now it's important. Or God may show us a pattern of sin we've lived with for decades. We may have excused others' lies, blamed people for our anger, or denied our neglect of those we claim to love. Whatever God reveals, it's time to do something about it. Don't run from the truth. Be honest. Own it.

Confess it to God.

All sin is first against God. It says, "My way is better than your way. I know more than you know. My will is more important than your will." So our response of confession must first be addressed to God. King David committed adultery and murder. In his famous confession in the Psalms, he wrote, "For I know my transgressions, and my sin is always before me. Against you, you only, have I sinned and done what is evil in your sight" (Ps. 51:3-4). Wait! What about the woman and the dead guy? Yes, David had to be honest with the people he betrayed, but his first stop was the throne of God.

Take the steps.

All repentance involves concrete steps of faith. If we've hurt someone, we go to that person and ask for forgiveness. If someone has hurt us and we've harbored bitterness, we choose to forgive just as Christ forgave us. If we've stolen something, we give it back or pay for it. If we've been engaged in gossip, we choose gratitude when we speak of people from now on. If involved with pornography, we install software that blocks those sites. If we've spent too much time at work instead of being home with our spouse and kids, we rearrange our priorities.

Create new habits.

Most of our sins aren't isolated instances. They're deeply ingrained thoughts, desires, perceptions, and behaviors. Repentance is a turning—a turning *from* the sin and a turning *toward* kindness, justice, and righteousness. Almost always, repentance involves replacing old patterns of thinking with new, godly ones. Some experts claim that new habits take at least twenty-one days to establish. That's a good rule of thumb. We need concerted, disciplined effort to do the right thing for at least twenty-one days so that the new behavior becomes a habit. And many of us need even more help—we need a trusted friend to talk to us, pray for us, and hold us accountable.

Never forget.

God has called you to live according to your new identity as a chosen, adopted, forgiven child of the King. He has made you his masterpiece, created to represent him in all you are and all you do. In this life, we're still flawed, and we have desires that are contrary to God's best. We need constant corrections to keep coming back. This isn't a game we can afford to lose. We're partners with God to reshape our lives to bring honor to him and have a positive impact on the people in our world.

THINK ABOUT IT . . .

Remember the joy of God's forgiveness and become skilled at the fine art of repentance.

1. How would you describe the differences between "godly sorrow" and "worldly sorrow"? Which one better describes how you've related to sin and to God? Explain your answer.

2. How does your view of God influence your willingness to repent?

3. What difference would it make (or does it make) to follow the recommendations at the end of the chapter?

Lord Jesus, bring me out of denial and shame. Show me the wonder of your grace so I'll be eager to repent. Thank you for the truth of your Word, the voice of your Spirit, and the love of those who have the courage to tell me the truth.

GO DEEPER . . .

1. What does Titus 3:3-8 say about your identity in Christ?

2. How does Col. 3:12-17 describe God's purpose for you?

3. How does James 1:2-8 show you how to stand strong and stay on track?

CHAPTER 5

SALT AND LIGHT

You can give without loving.
But you can't love without giving.

—AMY CARMICHAEL

A few years ago, a city alderman who had held the position for sixteen years was considering retirement. As was customary in city politics, the alderman was given the privilege to appoint his successor. My name was put forward, and I was vetted by the city council. Of course, they asked members of the community to voice their opinions about my qualifications and character. Members of the LGBTQ community (lesbian, gay, bi-sexual, transgender, queer) had strenuous objections, so I offered to meet with them. I hosted about twenty-five from their group at a restaurant. I went by myself because I didn't want them to feel outnumbered or threatened in any way.

I briefly introduced myself, and I invited them to ask any question on their minds. For the next hour, they asked dozens of questions about me, my views, and our church. One of them asked if we would revise our church website to say that we support the LGBTQ community, replacing our stated belief that God's design for marriage is between a man and a woman. I wasn't defensive or angry. I simply told them, "No, we won't do that. We won't change our beliefs so I can become an alderman."

At the end of the hour, I had listened carefully to their points of view, and I stated mine without raising my voice or arguing with them. But there was no question where I stood on the issues they felt strongly about. Several of them were obviously angry at my responses. One man in particular was loud, demanding, and critical of every answer I gave. At the end of our time, I said, "You say you stand for inclusion and tolerance, but it appears you're intolerant of my faith. That seems to be inconsistent." I wasn't asking for a response or provoking an argument. I was simply stating an observation about the inconsistency in his position, and I hoped at least some of those present would understand.

At the end of the meeting, a lady stood up and told the group, "I don't know the reverend very well, but I trust him, and I plan to vote for him." But for the first time in Mayor Daley's history as mayor, he didn't appoint the person nominated for the post of alderman. I was turned down, but that's not the end of the story.

Three years later, my assistant Veronica told me a man named Felix wanted to see me. I didn't recognize his name, but I was glad to meet him. It turned out I *had* met him before—at the meeting with the LGBTQ community. It was the man who had been so angry and defiant during the meeting, although now his demeanor was very different. He smiled and said,

"Pastor Choco, you may not remember me. I'm leaving the city of Chicago, but before I go, I wanted to see you. I've trusted Jesus Christ as my Savior, and I wanted you to know that God has done great things in my life. God told me that before I leave, I need to make things right with you." He began crying as he spoke to me. He paused for a second, and then he asked, "Would you forgive me for being so obnoxious to you? I said things about you and your church that weren't true."

I hugged him, "Brother, I forgave you years ago, and I'm thrilled to hear that you've come to know Jesus! I'm so happy to hear about your journey!"

Felix is still an activist, but now he's an activist for Jesus. He writes a blog about the grace and power of God to transform lives. He gives all the glory to God, and he generously mentions that I was kind to him when he was angry with me. Felix's sister is now visiting our church. But those aren't the only lives God touched as a result of that meeting three years earlier. The lady who had been the president of the LGBTQ organization is now on our missions team and is a Life Group coach. She is living a life of abstinence, walking with God in power and love.

We don't demand that people stop struggling with temptation. All of us have temptations and propensities to sin. They may take the form of homosexual urges, adulterous desires, addictions, deep-seated bitterness, greed, gluttony, or any other number of other damaging inclinations. *Being* tempted isn't a sin; *giving in* to the temptation is the sin. We love sinners because we're sinners and Jesus loves us. We have every right to speak the truth, but if we grasp God's grace at all, we won't despise sinners. Rather, our hearts will be broken by sin—both ours and theirs.

We can have the kind of impact Jesus had on people only when we grasp the fact that his kingdom is very different from the world around us. In fact, it appears to be upside down.

THE UPSIDE-DOWN KINGDOM

Jesus made a number of dramatic statements that blew people away, but sometimes we tend to get so familiar with them that they lose their punch. Before we can have a profoundly positive influence on people, we need to go back to those windows to see Jesus' heart and his relationships. He calls us to live every day in his upside-down kingdom.

As we've seen, the world where we live values intelligence, power, and riches. Every moment of every day, the people around us eagerly pursue success, pleasure, and approval. They compare themselves with others, and they're never satisfied. These pursuits may excite us for a moment, but they inevitably leave us empty, alone, and desperate.

Jesus offers depths of meaning and heights of joy, but from a very different source. Jesus was countercultural in his day, and his message is still jarring in ours. Let me paraphrase some of his bold statements:

"Those who try to find their lives will lose them, but those who lose their lives for my sake will find them."

"The last shall be first, and the first shall be last."

"The way to gain power is to be a servant of all."

"The way to have true riches is to be radically generous."

"To have honor, care for the lost and the least."

"To experience the fullness of forgiveness, be brutally honest about your sin."

"The proud will be humbled, and the humble will be exalted."

"The way to true freedom is to be God's slave."

"Being religious only makes you brittle, judgmental, and self-righteous, but grace gives you a blend of tenderness and strength."

If Christ lives in us, controlling our personalities, we will leave glorious marks on the lives we touch. Not because of our lovely characters, but because of his.

—EUGENIA PRICE

The American dream is to have it all; the kingdom dream is to lose it all. This doesn't mean we have to give everything away, but it means we need to hold everything the world values—money, prestige, popularity, comfort—so lightly that it has no hold on us. It means we realize everything in our lives is a gift from God to be used for one purpose: his glory.

To make a difference in the lives of others, we first have to realize God's kingdom is different from what most people assume—perhaps the polar opposite. We first have to think of Christ himself: he had it all, but he gave it all up for our benefit. The one who created the universe and lived in unimaginable splendor didn't destroy us when we turned our backs on him. He became one of us, was born in a stable, and gave his life in our place to bring us back to God. He lived the life we could never live, and he died the death we should have died. His kindness and love, as well as his wisdom and power, are like nothing in our world. He turned the world upside down, and we need to see ourselves and others from his point of view.

AN UPSIDE-DOWN LIFE

First-century Palestine was, in many ways, very different from our world of modern technology and conveniences, but one thing hasn't changed in two millennia: human nature. The Romans valued power, wealth, and beauty, and they despised weakness, generosity, and poverty. The Jewish leaders weren't much better. They knew God's laws, yet they used their leadership positions to intimidate and dominate. When Jesus began his most famous message, the Sermon on the Mount, he broke the mold for their culture . . . and for ours.

In a series of statements at the beginning of the sermon, Jesus outlined a very different agenda for people who follow him. Each sentence begins with the word "blessed," so the statements are collectively called "The Beatitudes." The first one must have shocked the people who were listening: "Blessed are the poor in spirit, for theirs is the kingdom of heaven" (Matt. 5:3). Who has access to the riches of God's kingdom? Only those who admit they are utterly bankrupt without his grace. But Jesus didn't stop there. He taught that what God values are the things most of us avoid at all costs: mourning, humility, hungering more for God than for prime rib or a great pork chop (a "chuleta" at my family table), mercy for outcasts, purity of heart, making peace instead of demanding our way, being so committed to God that we suffer any consequences, and even rejoicing in mistreatment because we realize God's heroes have always been persecuted.

The Beatitudes restructure our hearts and our values. How? By showing us how we fall so far short of these traits. If we're honest about what's in our hearts and our behavior, we have to admit there's far more pride and self-pity than humility, more self-absorption than mercy for hurting people, very mixed

thoughts and desires instead of purity, and a radical commitment to comfort instead of a willingness to suffer for God's
cause. And if we're still honest, most of us have to admit that
we sure hope God grades on a curve! We hope he gives us a
pass because we've done a few good things even though there
are plenty of red Xs on our score sheet.

But God doesn't grade on a curve. At the beginning of the
sermon, Jesus is showing us that we are helpless and hopeless
apart from the grace of God. Our first choice, then, is to throw
ourselves wholly on the mercy of the one who lived a perfect life
and died to forgive us, the one who is committed to change us
from the inside out.

The Christian life isn't a self-improvement project. God
doesn't expect us to try as hard as we can and see what
happens. He has given us the greatest security and power in the
universe to transform us and equip us—he has given us himself.
Jesus completely fulfilled the qualifications of the Beatitudes,
and he creates those rare qualities in us as we trust him. Jesus
emptied himself; the king of all became a pauper to make us
royalty in his kingdom. Jesus wept at Lazarus's tomb. He was so
consumed with sharing himself with the woman at the well that
he didn't notice he'd missed lunch. In the gospels, we see him
constantly reaching out to the outcasts of society: lepers, the
lame, the blind, the old, foreigners, prostitutes, and women. He
spent nights in prayer communing with his Father. He suffered
brutal torture so we could have God's peace. And he valued us
so much he was glad to go to the cross to suffer and die in our
place.

Jesus isn't asking us to do anything he hasn't already done.
But he's more than a good example to follow. As we're amazed

at his love and power, he radically transforms our hearts, our motivations, and our relationships.

How do people live who have a restructured heart and values consistent with God and his kingdom? What kind of impact will they have on the people around them? Jesus used two very descriptive metaphors: salt and light. Both are necessary for life. He explained:

> "You are the salt of the earth. But if the salt loses its saltiness, how can it be made salty again? It is no longer good for anything, except to be thrown out and trampled underfoot. You are the light of the world. A town built on a hill cannot be hidden. Neither do people light a lamp and put it under a bowl. Instead they put it on its stand, and it gives light to everyone in the house. In the same way, let your light shine before others, that they may see your good deeds and glorify your Father in heaven." (Matt. 5:13-16)

Words can never adequately convey the incredible impact of our attitudes toward life. The longer I live the more convinced I become that life is 10 percent what happens to us and 90 percent how we respond to it.

—CHUCK SWINDOLL

SALT

I enjoy watching Robert Irvine on his show, *Restaurant Impossible*. In every episode, he walks into a restaurant that's in financial trouble and often run by people on the brink of emotional exhaustion. He talks to them about their menu, their staffing, and the process of cooking each dish. Quite often, Irvine and the owners rebuild the interiors while they revamp everything else. It's a "total makeover" in only a few days! Most of the owners don't really know why they're failing to attract and keep customers. Irvine has to show them the underlying reason: the food is awful! In almost every episode, he has a simple but effective recommendation: use a little more salt. That seems to fix everything!

Everyone knows that salt adds flavor, but some believe it only enhances the flavors already present in the food. Research shows, however, that salt works by suppressing bitterness, which releases the other flavors that had been masked.[14] When Jesus reminds believers that *we* are salt, it means we are to suppress our own bitterness toward those who are above us, below us, or competing with us, and our love for them suppresses their bitterness toward God and others.

In the ancient world, salt was a precious commodity. It was like gold—those who had it were considered rich. In fact, the English word *salary* means "salt money." A person who isn't valuable is said to be "not worth his salt." Why is salt valuable?

- It preserves meat so it doesn't decompose.
- It suppresses bitter flavors so food tastes better.
- It cleanses and purifies.
- It's essential for bodily health and healing.[15]

By acting as salt in our world, we help stop the inevitable decay of those around us into hopelessness, selfishness, and destruction. Without our influence, they only become more self-absorbed, confused, and angry.

Yet when we look around today, we still see plenty of decay. What's the matter? Are Christians not having any influence? Rest assured, without the powerful impact of believers, this world would be in far worse condition. We have a pervasive and positive impact on every social structure and segment of society, but our work isn't done. The drift is always toward rot and decay, and we need to get out of the saltshaker so the character of Christ can flow from us into our family members, friends, neighbors, coworkers, and everyone else we meet each day.

Salt preserves and flavors, but it can lose its effectiveness. When this happens, it becomes useless and fails to suppress bitterness in our most important relationships. Jesus taught: "Salt is good, but if it loses its saltiness, how can you make it salty again? Have salt among yourselves, and be at peace with each other" (Mark 9:50). This is a warning: don't stop being salty! How can we know if our salt is still effective? The measurement is whether our presence and words suppress bitterness and promote peace, or they shatter peace and enflame bitterness.

What kind of impact are you having on people?

LIGHT

In the grace of God, he is willing to turn darkness into brilliant, beautiful light. In our church, we've seen it countless times. A few years ago a single mom came to our church with her two teenagers. Her life was a mess. A painful divorce and drugs had devastated her. Her son Orlando was eighteen and her daughter Angelique was seventeen. The kids sensed genuine love in the people in our youth group, and they began attending regularly. They couldn't get enough! When they heard about our discipleship program called the Chicago Master's Commission, both of them signed up. They wanted to be part of a community of people who were diving deep into the heart of God and were committed to make a difference.

They graduated after three years and were ready to devote their lives to serve God. At the time, we were opening a shelter for homeless men, and we asked Orlando to be in charge of it. He was only twenty-one, but we saw greatness in him. Orlando treated the men and the volunteers with a wonderful blend of kindness and firmness. He had a profound impact on family members who had struggled with poverty and drugs. His mother eventually came to the Chicago Dream Center, a recovery home for women caught in a life of prostitution or drug addiction and women who have been abused as sex slaves . . . and God turned her life around in that center for restoration and hope.

We opened another church campus in Chicago and we asked Orlando to go there to lead the youth ministry. He is pouring himself into those kids, sharing the heart and skills he learned in Master's Commission. After a while, his mother graduated from the Dream Center and the offsite residential site, The Farm. She's off drugs, she's walking with the Lord, she has the support of her faith community, and she has a good job. The transformation from darkness to light is remarkable.

Orlando was recently commissioned and anointed as a pastor in our church leadership, and the impact of his life continues to expand. Angelique is serving at the same church where Orlando is a pastor. This brother and sister are having a profound impact on their entire family. In addition to their mother's progress, their father has come out of the shadows and is now attending church, and their older sister is also attending and becoming increasingly involved in missions. Before Orlando and Angelique came to our church with their mother, they lived in the darkness of a hopeless home, but they became beacons of hope for everyone around them.

In the New Testament, we find three "God is" statements: Jesus told the woman at the well, "God is spirit" (John 4:24); John tells us, "God is love" (1 John 4:8); and John also explains, "God is light" (1 John 1:5). And of course, Jesus made the bold claim, "I am the light of the world" (John 8:12; 9:5). Throughout the Bible, the light of God symbolizes his infinite knowledge because nothing is hidden from his sight, and it points to God's perfect purity. Light is an essential attribute of a holy, righteous, infinitely perfect God . . . so it's surprising when Jesus turns to us and announces, "You are the light of the world." We are to be like Christ, and our impact is to be like his.

How can we be lights in the dark world around us? Jesus tells us, "Let your light shine before others, that they may see your good deeds and glorify your Father in heaven" (Matt. 5:16). When we love, give, and serve with hearts overflowing with gratitude, people notice—and they instantly realize that's not normal! These rare attitudes and behaviors are at odds with what they see in the world. All around them, they see selfishness, resentment, and competition to get more power, prestige, and possessions. When they see our blend of love and strength shining like lights, they're amazed, and hopefully, they'll be attracted to the source of the light they see in us: Jesus himself.

Jesus explained that light is only effective if it shines openly and brightly. He used the metaphor of a city on a hill (Matt. 5:14). Then and today, most cities were built in valleys near rivers and streams. But Jesus was saying that his people are to be different. He wants us to step away from the convenient, the expected, and the normal—and stand out so we can be seen from miles around.

To make a similar point, he used another metaphor—a lampstand (Matt. 5:15). In a room lit only by a candle, it makes no sense to put that candle under a bowl or basket. Instead, it's put high on a stand to illuminate every corner of the room. His point is clear: too often those who claim to follow God aren't shining brightly, and they aren't illuminating every aspect of family and community life. In a dark room, people stumble over the furniture and each other, getting hurt and inflicting wounds on each other. That's a picture of the impact of darkness in relationships devoid of God's light.

Light is an essential aspect of the nature of God, and it's the nature of his people to shine like lights, too. But too often, we fail. We can point to three common reasons we hide our light under a bowl:

1. *We don't want to be exposed.* We simply have too many things we want to hide, or there's one huge thing we've done that haunts us with shame. We'd rather keep our secrets and hide the truth, even at the expense of missing the privilege of being a light for God.

2. *We don't want the inconvenience.* A commitment to love the unlovely, give sacrificially, and serve in obscurity takes a toll of time and energy. These activities cut into our self-absorbed priorities.

3. *We don't want to lose control.* Oh, we're glad to stand up for God when it's our decision and it promotes our agendas, but Jesus' command to "Follow me" is not just for when it's convenient. When Jesus said those words to Peter, Andrew, James, and John, they left their boats and nets to join him. When he said those words to Matthew, he left his profitable

tax business to be fully and instantly committed to Jesus. In the same way, when we say "yes" to him, we put ourselves in his hands. In the final analysis, all of us have a choice every moment of every day: Will we say to God, "Not my will, but yours," or, "Not your will, but mine."

Calling is a "yes" to God that carries a "no" to the chaos of modern demands. Calling is the key to tracing the story line of our lives and unriddling the meaning of our existence in a chaotic world.

—OS GUINNESS

When our church began to reach out to needy people in our community, we didn't have to look very far to find them. Our church was small, so we purchased an apartment building we could convert into facilities we could use. Our board met and decided to use the bottom floor as a fellowship center for the members of the church. After some major renovations that included new walls, paint, and carpeting, we were ready for the grand opening. The week before we scheduled our first event, I met with a representative from the city's Department of Human Resources. He explained that more shelters were needed for the Hispanic population on the north side of Chicago . . . our side of town.

At that moment, I realized I had to decide what kind of church we'd be. Were we going to spend our resources on ourselves and become a comfortable club, or would we swing our doors open to the destitute people who needed food, clothing, and housing? When I suggested we revise our plans for the fellowship center to convert it into a shelter, the light of God's truth shined brightly to reveal that we weren't a compassionate group of leaders. I met stiff resistance to my plan at first, but after much prayer and many conversations, the board decided to be salt to stop the decay in our community and light to show the love of God to the hungry, the poor, and the disenfranchised.

A new adventure unfolded in front of us. We had no clue what it meant to host a shelter for homeless people, but we gave it our all. We bought beds, prepared a kitchen, and trained staff and volunteers to meet needs with cheerful hearts.

When the first person came in off the streets, the look in her eyes told us we had accomplished God's goal: She was thrilled and amazed! I'm not sure she would have been happier if we'd put her up in a five-star hotel! She stayed with us for two months, but then she died of AIDS. I don't know the details of her life before she came through our doors, but the months she stayed with us were filled with joy, laughter, and love.

Opening the shelter changed many lives of poor people in our community, but it did more than that: it changed our church. Our people caught the fire of compassion, and they burned brightly in countless ways. Being the light of the world meant caring for the people on the streets in our neighborhood, not in theory, but in hands-on, practical demonstrations of the love of Jesus. Doing good was a way to be salt and light to the people who came to us, and it compelled our people to reassess our values, our priorities, and our hearts. The people of our church are genuinely excited to be salt to stop the decay, and light to show the love of Christ.

All of us face choices each day, to hide in darkness or come into the light of God's truth and love. And those who have experienced God's light also have a choice, to let it be hidden by the worries and distractions of the world, or to hold Jesus up and let his light shine through our efforts to care for others. When Paul wrote his sweeping letter about God's purposes to the people of Ephesus, he told them to remember where they'd come from:

> For you were once darkness, but now you are light in the Lord. Live as children of light (for the fruit of the light consists in all goodness, righteousness and truth) and find out what pleases the Lord. Have nothing to do with the fruitless deeds of darkness, but rather expose them. (Eph. 5:8-11)

As we shine like stars in the dark night of our culture, we can expect various responses: many people will be drawn to the light and find the love of Jesus, a few will criticize us for doing what they aren't willing to do, and others will simply ignore us. But one thing is sure: God will be pleased. We need to stay on guard, however, because darkness always threatens to overwhelm us. The prince of darkness isn't tired and he isn't finished. He will try to discourage and distract us so we'll forget that we have the incredible privilege and responsibility to represent our Creator, King, and Savior to a lost, dying, and dark world.

Let me offer a few suggestions:

- Be honest about how you and your church may be contributing to decay and darkness through bad attitudes and selfish behaviors. No, it's not fun to let the light of Christ shine into the deep recesses of your soul, but it's necessary to see what's hidden there.

- Think of a person whom you don't want to be around. Let love suppress the bitterness, first in you, and then hopefully in him or her as you patiently shake the salt of grace into that person's life.

- For one hour a day during the next week, live by the Golden Rule: treat others with the same love and respect you'd like to receive from them. If you can do it for an hour a day for a week, you might be able to create a new habit of being light to those around you.

As we trust God to make us salty and bright, we have to remain vigilant, and we have to support each other in this great endeavor. Where we find conflict, God has called us to be peacemakers. Where we find people suffering, we are ministers of Christ to bind up their wounds. Where we find hatred, we share the transforming love of Christ and return good for evil. When we find selfishness, we pour out ourselves in glad sacrifice to care for others.

That's what it means to be salt and light. It's God's calling, it's our struggle, and it's our pleasure.

Sometimes the impact of living as light and salt can be felt in the church as the body of Christ gathers together. Recently, I met with a gentleman who is running for a seat in a local election, and he described his experience when he visited our church. He explained that he had been standing outside next to a tree we'd planted. As he greeted people and shook their hands, he had a strange sensation. He hadn't planned on attending the worship service—his plan was just to meet people so they'd recognize his face and name when they entered the voting booth. But in those personal interchanges with our people, he felt compelled to go inside to see what had made such a difference in their lives. During the service, he felt a presence, a light, and a sense of peace he had never experienced before. He told me, "Pastor, it became clear to me that there are two different worlds, and I was living in the wrong one." (He was referring to the political world as a world of darkness.) The love he sensed from our people was so attractive that he instantly realized that's what he wanted to experience. Light and salt changed the direction of his life: The next day he went to his campaign office and fired half his staff. He explained that he felt he needed to remove some of the negative influences surrounding him. Talk about having an impact!

THINK ABOUT IT . . .

Remember that Jesus has already put salt and light in you by his grace. Let the love of God suppress bitterness and shine for everyone to see.

1. Why is it so much easier to enflame bitterness instead of suppressing it with the love of God? In what ways does bitterness seem attractive? What are some costs of harboring resentment and hatred?

2. What are some acts of service you can perform today to be light in a dark world? What can your church do in your community?

3. Does it scare you or thrill you to think of actually living by the Golden Rule for an hour a day for a week? Explain your answer.

Lord Jesus, your love suppresses bitterness in me, and your light reveals both my sin and your grace. Show me how I can be saltier and brighter today.

GO DEEPER . . .

1. What does 1 Cor. 6:19-20 say about your identity in Christ?

2. How does Eph. 2:8-10 describe God's purpose for you?

3. How does 2 Tim. 1:8-14 show you how to stand strong and stay on track?

CHAPTER 6

MOVE IN CLOSER

We are the Bibles the world is reading;
We are the creeds the world is needing;
We are the sermons the world is heeding.

—BILLY GRAHAM

It was a moment of crisis. God's people were afraid they were losing their identity, their place in society, the rights they had come to expect. The government wanted to minimize the influence of their faith, and some of their spiritual leaders recommended they fight back or run away. The people were confused and discouraged. They didn't know which way to turn.

Does this sound familiar? Many Christians are having this debate today about conditions in our culture, but I'm describing a crisis of faith that occurred twenty-six centuries ago. The Babylonians had attacked Judah and destroyed the temple in Jerusalem. The temple was much more than a building: it was the center of worship and the source of identity for the people of God. Even worse, the Babylonians had carried away most of the valuable and irreplaceable sacred items along with many of the Jewish people. The exiles felt demoralized because their way of life, their traditions, and their hopes to live in a godly nation seemed ruined. The Babylonian rulers expected the Jews to blend in like the people from all the other conquered nations.

A prophet named Hananiah had a different plan. He advised the people to be patient and wait it out, that within two years the Babylonian yoke would be broken and all would be well (Jer. 28). Implicit in his message was the instruction to avoid contact with Babylonian society so they could remain pure in their faith and practices. It was, he assured them, the only way for them to keep their identity and walk with God.

But God, through his faithful prophet Jeremiah, exposed Hananiah as a false prophet and liar. Jeremiah delivered God's real (and surprising) message:

> This is what the Lord Almighty, the God of Israel, says to all those I carried into exile from Jerusalem to Babylon: "Build houses and settle down; plant gardens and eat what they produce. Marry and have sons and daughters; find wives for your sons and give your daughters in marriage, so that they too may have sons and daughters. Increase in number there; do not decrease. Also, seek the peace and prosperity of the city to which I have carried you into exile. Pray to the Lord for it, because if it prospers, you too will prosper." (Jer. 29:4-7)

Yes, the Babylonian yoke would be broken, but it would be *seventy* years later, not two (Jer. 29:10). In the meantime, God was telling the people to settle in and make Babylon their home, to live there and not try to leave as soon as possible. Instead of hating the pagan city, he told them to "seek the peace and prosperity of the city" and pray for it. His promise was that if the city prospered, God's people would benefit, too.

God warned the people not to listen to false prophets who told them to work for the city's destruction. Then God gave them a promise many Christians today can recite from memory: "'For I know the plans I have for you,' declares the Lord, 'plans to prosper you and not to harm you, plans to give you hope and a future'" (Jer. 29:11). But most Christians aren't aware of the context, the command, and the promises leading up to this magnificent verse. God's plans were very different from those proposed by the Babylonian rulers or the false prophets. His plan—for them and for us—is to live among the unbelievers in their cities to bless people there.

What does it mean to live in our cities today and be a blessing? It means we don't complain about everything we don't like, but instead we get involved and act as salt and light for the people and institutions. We actively serve the needy and protect the oppressed. We work for justice with our police departments and courts. We support the arts so culture flourishes, and in everything we do, we provide light to share the gospel with anyone who will listen. If we serve, work, protect, and love the people of our communities, they'll know we're not standing outside condemning them, and we're not running to get away from them—we're their friends and partners to make our neighborhoods and cities better places for everybody. We earn their trust, so they're more likely to listen to our perspectives.

God's message to his people in Babylon was the same as it is to us today. It would be easy to just blend in and accept the moral slide of our culture, and it's tempting to rally behind some of our loud and angry religious leaders who demand our rights in an us-vs.-them showdown. But those aren't God's solutions, and those reactions don't lead to God's blessings. God wants us to roll up our sleeves and get involved. If we do, we'll have to trust him more than ever, and we'll be stretched to the limit of our resources, but we'll also experience God's presence and power. He promises to bless us if we'll get involved in being a blessing to the people, institutions, and organizations in our cities.

Too often today, believers are responding with fear when they should respond with faith. God is calling us—you and me—to the most challenging task of our lives: to engage the difficult people around us and the most difficult problems in our culture with a beautiful and all-too-rare blend of kindness and unwavering truth. He is calling us to be more like Jesus, to be countercultural and live an upside-down life of humility, compassion for the poor, justice for the oppressed, and integrity in every aspect of daily living: our words, our money, our sex lives, and everything else.

Jesus calls us to be like him, living in righteousness and justice—both, not one or the other. In the Bible, *justice* involves two activities: punishing the guilty and caring for the poor. In America, we usually focus only the first aspect of justice. We need to support law enforcement, but we need to do more . . . much more. We need to care for the poor, the homeless, the hungry, and the victims of crime.

In response to the violence in the city of Chicago, our church inaugurated a "Safety in the Sanctuary Initiative" to build bridges between the church and the community . . . and even between the community and the Chicago Police Department. In January

2016, our church opened its doors for three weeks to people who had nowhere to go. We served family meals, offered after-school tutoring, and provided shelter from the cold. Our efforts required a higher level of service than we'd ever seen in our staff members and volunteers, but this initiative re-awakened our commitment to engage the community in love. We are the church, and we are called to love.

Only Jesus would be crazy enough to suggest that if you want to become the greatest, you should become the least.

—SHANE CLAIBORNE

In the previous chapter we looked at the fact *that* we are salt and light; in this chapter, we'll examine *how* we function as salt and light in our world. As we will see, we answer God's call in three widening circles: personal relationships, our community, and the world.

All of us know people who are struggling. Whether they are rich or poor, young or old, white, black, Hispanic, Asian, or some other ethnic group, we come face to face every day with those whose hearts are broken. People all around us are struggling with addiction, divorce, disease, death, financial worries, prodigal children, abuse, abandonment, and a host of other devastating problems. We walk past or work next to people who carry these enormous burdens—in their own lives or in their closest relationships—but we may not even know it unless we take time to get to know them.

In our cities and towns, we encounter classes, races, and groups of people who feel abandoned and disenfranchised. If we look hard enough and drive around long enough, we'll find pockets of poverty, hunger, and homelessness even in the most affluent communities.

In our country and the wider world, the movement away from Christian values seems like a massive snowball halfway down the hill and picking up speed. We don't know what to do (and our leaders don't seem to have any good answers) about problems in race relations, immigration, the plight of refugees, the massive and sudden shift toward same-sex marriage, the proliferation of gun violence, climate change, and the recent but terrifying reality of terrorism. God wants us to step into those very problems.

We step into these problems with a blend of godly wisdom and courage. For instance, we sometimes hear politicians and other leaders who have radical (and radically wrong) solutions to the problem of immigration. Their answer is to say an emphatic "No!" to everyone standing at our borders. We've seen near-riots break out in the Southwest as mothers tried to save their children from oppression, danger, and death in Central American countries. I want to ask these protesters, "How can you argue about children crossing the border? Why are you so afraid?" It only takes a little humanity to empathize with these desperate mothers.

We need to be honest about our human tendency to react in fear and anger instead of responding with grace and power. If we accommodate the problems and just "go with the flow," we'll find ways to avoid stepping into others' personal problems because they are too messy, and we'll accept cultural shifts as the new norm because "everybody has a right to their opinions."

Angry people get the most publicity and news coverage, but I believe there are far more people in our churches who are simply overwhelmed by others' problems—in their families and friendships, in the local community, and in the wider world—and no one notices when they give up and withdraw. One man had been fiercely critical of any politician or Christian leader who would even talk to an opponent. He said sadly, "What's the use? I was driving myself to a heart attack or a stroke by being so angry all the time, but I wasn't making any difference—except making everybody close to me miserable. I've given up . . . on our country, on our leaders, on myself, and to be honest, on God."

MOVING IN . . . GRACEFULLY

If we accommodate, attack, or withdraw, we won't have any significant impact on our family, friends, communities, or the wider world. Engaging with others means we may be repulsed by the messiness we find, and we may face opposition, but God wants us to keep moving toward people, not standing above them to condemn them and not running away to avoid getting involved. We need to remember that Jesus stepped out of the splendor of heaven to become one of us, and he is calling us to step out of our comfort zones to identify so closely with hurting, disagreeable people that they're convinced we care for them.

Physicist Albert Einstein remarked, "The world is a dangerous place to live; not because of the people who are evil, but because of the people who don't do anything about it." English philosopher Edmund Burke commented, "The only thing necessary for the triumph [of evil] is for good men to do nothing." And Martin Luther King, Jr. observed, "He who passively accepts evil is as much involved in it as he who helps to perpetrate it. He who accepts evil without protesting against it is really cooperating with it." So if we truly care about others, we don't have the choice to close our eyes or walk away.

The Bible constantly challenges people to stop being self-absorbed and to reach out to care for the unfortunate. Let me cite only three examples:

- The prophet Isaiah watched as God's people performed religious duties (fasting, specifically) without a heart of love. Rituals alone aren't enough. We need to be generous for the right reasons. God promised the blessing of his presence if the people obeyed with their whole hearts:

    "Is not this the kind of fasting I have chosen:
    to loose the chains of injustice
    and untie the cords of the yoke,
    to set the oppressed free
    and break every yoke?

    Is it not to share your food with the hungry
    and to provide the poor wanderer with shelter—
    when you see the naked, to clothe them,
    and not to turn away from your own flesh and blood?

    Then your light will break forth like the dawn,
    and your healing will quickly appear;
    then your righteousness will go before you,
    and the glory of the LORD will be your rear guard.

    Then you will call, and the LORD will answer;
    you will cry for help, and he will say: Here am I."
    (Isa. 58:6-9)

• The prophet Zechariah recorded God's heart for the vulnerable and his expectation that we would join him in providing for them: "This is what the LORD Almighty said: 'Administer true justice; show mercy and compassion to one another. Do not oppress the widow or the fatherless, the foreigner or the poor. Do not plot evil against each other" (Zech. 7:9-10).

In his book, *Generous Justice*, pastor Tim Keller applies this passage to Christians living in our modern world:

> In premodern, agrarian societies, these four groups [in Zechariah 7] had no social power. They lived at subsistence level and were only days from starvation if there was any famine, invasion, or even minor social unrest. Today this quartel would be expanded to include the refugee, the migrant worker, the homeless, and many single parents and elderly people.[16]

Sadly, the people didn't listen to God's challenge: "But they refused to pay attention; stubbornly they turned their backs and covered their ears. They made their hearts as hard as flint and would not listen to the law or to the words that the Lord Almighty had sent by his Spirit through the earlier prophets. So the LORD Almighty was very angry" (Zech. 7:11-12).

Are we doing any better?

• The same themes carry through to the New Testament. James wrote to describe what a gospel-drenched life looks like in practical experience. It's not enough, he explained, to just believe the right doctrines and attend enough services. Genuine faith is lived out in sacrifice and service to the most vulnerable among us. New Testament usage of the word "religion" usually means spiritual activities devoid of God's love and purpose, but James redefines the word and infuses it with meaning. He told his readers in the first century, and God shouts it to us today: "Religion that God our Father accepts as pure and faultless is this: to look after orphans and widows in their distress and to keep oneself from being polluted by the world" (James 1:27).

We have better news to report about the Christians in the first centuries. When two plagues ravaged the Roman world in the second and third centuries, almost a third of the entire population perished. The first plague, probably smallpox, began in 165 when Marcus Aurelius was the emperor. The second one, in 251, may have been a measles outbreak.

In each of these plagues, the pagans prayed to their gods and looked to their doctors for help, but the doctors left town to save themselves. Many family members were terrified and left infected brothers, sisters, parents, and children to die. Without nursing care, most of those who contracted the diseases died in excruciating pain.

The Christians, though, didn't run away. They stayed and doctored their own families, and they cared for the sick Roman families, too. A church leader, Dionysius, explained their motivation:

> Most of our brother Christians showed unbounded love and loyalty, never sparing themselves and

thinking only of one another. Heedless of danger, they took charge of the sick, attending to their every need and ministering to them in Christ, and with them departed this life serenely happy; for they were infected by others with the disease, drawing on themselves the sickness of their neighbors and cheerfully accepting their pains. Many, in nursing and curing others, transferred their death to themselves and died in their stead. . . . The best of our brothers lost their lives in this manner.[17]

Those Christians loved their sick, unbelieving neighbors as themselves—they were salt in a time of disease and decay, and they were light in the darkness of despair. In *The Rise of Christianity*, Rodney Stark concluded that the loving service of the Christians during those two plagues caused the number of believers to explode in the Roman Empire. How did it happen? Christians cared for their own family members instead of leaving them to die, so their mortality rate was significantly lower. And the Romans witnessed Christ's love in action! Within 200 years, the number of Christians increased from less than one percent to more than twenty-five percent of the empire. Because Christians risked death (and often suffered death) to serve people in their communities, Christianity became the dominant faith of the Roman Empire. The spread of Christianity wouldn't have happened if the believers hadn't risked their lives to care for the desperately sick people around them.[18]

James would have been—and Jesus is—proud of those believers.

These passages, and countless others, show us what it means to live out our new identity as God's chosen, forgiven, beloved children who have been given the monumental purpose of representing him to those around us. We are salt to arrest decay, and we are light to expose sin and illuminate God's forgiveness and a path of hope.

The process of salt curing is an ancient way to preserve meat and fish. Without it, the hams that dangle on hooks for months would stink and be inedible in only a few days at room temperature as bacteria and other organisms cause the meat to rot. The steps require careful preparation. Salt can be applied in three stages. The first stage takes about a month, the second about four days, and the last about two weeks. When the process is complete, the meat can last for more than a year.[19]

When we act as salt to the hurting people around us, we don't try to serve quickly and then leave them. We have to stay with it for a while, often a long while, to work the salt of God's love and truth deep into the other person. If we stop the process too soon (or if the other person stops it), the process of decay will begin again. Using too much salt can be a problem, but it isn't as bad as too little salt. A few problems in others' lives can be solved fairly quickly, but the devastating situations require time and unshakeable love to allow the salt of God's kindness and good purposes to work. In other words, be tenacious in your compassion!

The Christian is a person who makes it easy for others to believe in God.

—ROBERT MURRAY MCCHEYNE

Today, when we try to be light and salt, some listeners may wave their fingers at us and quote Jesus, "Do not judge, or you too will be judged" (Matt. 7:1). They assume that any comment that doesn't fully embrace another's opinions and choices is "judging," and therefore not right. The word "judge" has a range of meanings, from evaluation ("I didn't judge how long it would take me to get there") to condemnation (Jesus will return to judge evil and punish the wicked). A few sentences after this famous one-liner in the Sermon on the Mount, Jesus also says, "You hypocrite, first take the plank out of your own eye, and then you will see clearly to remove the speck from your brother's eye" (Matt. 7:5).

Here we see that judgment is necessary in order to "see clearly to remove the speck." Jesus' warning against judging certainly didn't mean that we shouldn't evaluate ideas, beliefs, and behaviors. God wants us to see things the way he sees them, and we are reminded of that fact on virtually every page of the Bible. Jesus also calls us to be "as shrewd as snakes and as innocent as doves" (Matt. 10:16). This means we are to evaluate according to the Bible's standards and communicate with kindness and love.

When anyone questions me about "judging" or "not judging," I calmly explain that judging is expected and even encouraged in the Scriptures. How else will we be able to recognize false prophets and false teachers? Jesus clearly said, "By their fruit you will recognize them" (Matt. 7:20). To recognize good or bad fruit, we have to evaluate (judge) the fruit. We can't judge a person's eternal salvation—that's left to God—but we can judge others' lives by their fruit.

The modern concept of tolerance says, "No one has the right to tell anyone else what's right and wrong." Jesus (as well as Moses, David, the prophets, Paul, Peter, the gospel writers, and every other author of Scripture) would disagree. We not only have the right to echo what the Bible says is right and wrong; we have an obligation to represent God to a fallen world. But our job is to evaluate and explain, not to condemn. When we point out sin, we need to speak out of sincere compassion for the sinner.

Light has a dual quality: it exposes danger and it reveals a way forward. When we find ourselves in a strange room at night, like getting up in the dark when we're staying at a friend's house, we can easily stumble over the furniture and get hurt. A simple flick of a switch shows us where everything is, allowing us to avoid tripping over clothes on the floor or the legs of chairs, as well as letting us see the clear path to the bathroom. When we are lights to the people in our lives, we serve both purposes: we gently and lovingly show them the dangers they face, and we offer a new way forward to different choices that promise hope, peace, and security.

When we follow God's calling to be salt and light, we don't manipulate others to earn accolades or gain power over them. We step into their lives from a position of security—we don't need anything from them; we only want to share the love, forgiveness, acceptance, hope, and strength we've received from God. We give with full hearts and open hands, letting people respond however they choose, and not taking it personally if they refuse our gracious offers.

INHERENT VALUE

It's easy to demonize people who have different values or who oppose our positions. Every night on the news, we have a front-row seat to watch the fierce fighting and name-calling between people on opposite sides of almost any issue. I'm not suggesting we all "just get along." That would be accommodating. No, I recommend that we hold fast to the truth God has given us, but his truth includes important insights: the inherent value of people. Every person on the planet—including the one who agrees with us and one who doesn't—is created in the image of God and is of invaluable worth: the richest and the poorest, Democrats and Republicans, immigrants and citizens, capitalists and socialists, insiders and outsiders . . . no one is excluded. God placed such a high value on every human being that he left heaven to make the ultimate sacrifice to save us.

When we talk with those who disagree with us, we need to listen carefully to fully understand their position. When we don't listen, we create two problems: we make assumptions, often wrong ones, about the other position, and we communicate that we don't care enough to value the other person's thoughts and values. If we don't listen, we lose the opportunity to connect with the person, no matter how right we believe our cause might be.

Quite often, we don't listen because we're reacting out of anger and fear that our way of life is being threatened. We're sure we're right and anyone who opposes us is obviously wrong . . . and probably evil, too! In the first century, Christians had a lot more to fear. They suffered persecution at the hands of the Romans and the Jews. Peter's first letter is a handbook on how to handle opposition. He encouraged his readers (and us): "Do not be frightened. But in your hearts revere Christ as Lord. Always be prepared to give an answer to everyone who asks you to give the reason for the hope that you have. But do this with gentleness and respect, keeping a clear conscience, so that those who speak maliciously against your good behavior in Christ may be ashamed of their slander" (1 Peter 3:14-16).

We may think we have to match *their* angry words with *our* angry words, but we don't. When people are set in their way of thinking, we need to be sensitive in our approach. A proverb gives us this insight: "Through patience a ruler can be persuaded, and a gentle tongue can break a bone" (Prov. 25:15). Solomon, the wise king, says that diplomacy, the careful choice of words, and an unthreatening demeanor can win a hearing from even the most powerful ruler—or a spouse, a parent, a child, a boss, or a neighbor. Solomon's proverb is a paradox: a gentle tongue has the power to break a strong bone. What does he mean? When people have taken a firm position, fierce opposition only makes them more entrenched and less willing to hear our reasoning. But if our words are encouraging and our demeanor is gentle, our message might break through to touch their hearts.

When I met with the twenty-five members of the local LGBTQ community, I didn't demand they agree with me. I didn't condemn them or accuse them. I wanted to represent Christ, and I thought about how he related to those who opposed him. He was very clear in his message to sinners, but they knew he loved them. That was my goal. I listened, and I told them what I believed. I was secure in my identity and my message, so I had no need to be defensive in any way. When the meeting was over, I had no guarantee God would use my "gentle tongue" to break down a hard heart or two in the group, but that's what he did.

Jesus was very gentle with the sick, the poor, and widows; he welcomed outcasts like the Samaritans, prostitutes, and tax collectors; and he was infinitely patient with his closest followers. The fiercest opposition was from the religious leaders who felt threatened by Jesus' new way to relate to God because they were going to lose power. With them, Jesus tried every communication technique. He met at night with Nicodemus, who didn't want his peers to know about the encounter. He openly corrected the misguided concepts of Pharisees who challenged his authority, and he bluntly warned the people who suffered under the leaders' oppression to avoid following their example. But Jesus also used an indirect method of persuasion.

In the opening verses of Jesus' most famous story about a lost sheep, a lost coin, and a lost son, Luke gives us the setting: "Now the tax collectors and sinners were all gathering around to hear Jesus. But the Pharisees and the teachers of the law muttered, 'This man welcomes sinners and eats with them'" (Luke 15:1-2). We usually think of the three parables as sweet stories about finding something or someone who was lost, but the main audience for those stories was the grumbling, self-righteous Pharisees. In the first two stories, the shepherd looks for the lost sheep and the woman looks for her lost coin. When we get to the third story, we see something very odd: no one goes to look for the lost son. Who should have gone? In that culture, everyone knew the answer to that question: the older brother.

In the story, the father represents God, the younger brother represents the tax collectors and sinners listening to Jesus, and the older brother represents the Pharisees. Instead of going out to find the sinners and bring them back to God, the religious leaders stood apart from them, judged them as inferior, and harshly condemned them—and they ridiculed Jesus for loving them, for being a true elder brother. In the parable's final scene, the father goes into the field to beg his angry son to come to the feast and celebrate the younger brother's return, but the older son is indignant. The father pleads, "My son, you are always with me, and everything I have is yours. But we had to celebrate and be glad, because this brother of yours was dead and is alive again; he was lost and is found" (Luke 15:31-32). The father used an affectionate term, "my son," (*teknon* in Greek) to gently, lovingly beg his son to come to the feast. If we understand the context, we realize Jesus is speaking directly to the judgmental Pharisees, tenderly asking them to come to the feast of God's love and forgiveness. His communication technique was brilliant and warm.

In the same way, we can learn to be diplomatic in our communication to win people's heart. Sadly, it doesn't always work. Jesus' beautiful story didn't have the impact he desired. The Pharisees standing around listening to the story didn't repent and join the feast of salvation. And no matter how diplomatic and prayerful we are, there are no guarantees people will respond to our message of love and hope.

What do you do with a man who is supposed to be the holiest man who has ever lived and yet goes around talking with prostitutes and hugging lepers? What do you do with a man who not only mingles with the most unsavory people but actually seems to enjoy them? The religious accused him of being a drunkard, a glutton and having tacky taste in friends. It is a profound irony that the Son of God visited this planet and one of the chief complaints against him was that he was not religious enough.

—REBECCA MANLEY PIPPERT

CONNECT

We can be salt and light in three spheres of relationships: we can connect with family, neighbors, friends, and coworkers we see regularly; our small groups and classes can take on projects that make a difference in the neighborhood; and our churches can tackle the big issues that threaten our communities, our nation, and our world. Let's look at each of these.

Personal impact

God has put each of us in a strategic position to touch particular lives. First, however, we need to take inventory of what's in our hearts. Admit your fears and your prejudices. Confess any self-righteousness and superiority to God, and thank him for his cleansing. Be honest about your anxiety in getting involved in the messiness of others' lives, and ask God to give you compassion and wisdom.

I know of a church where the preacher regularly condemns people who have tattoos. How many young people, especially young lost people, do you think feel welcomed there? Not many! Even if they don't have tats, many of their friends do. Don't be a Pharisee. Welcome people who don't look like you, don't talk like you, don't walk like you.

It's easy to label people as "liars," "fools," "stupid," or "jerks." When we make such hasty, black-or-white judgments about people, they remain objects that we then accept or reject. Instead, take the initiative to get to know other people, and learn to see them as complex, multidimensional characters—the way we want them to see us.

Let me offer some advice that I got from Rick Warren. He encouraged me to use the SPEAK method when I meet people. First, I ask them to share their *Story*. Then I ask, "What's your

Purpose in life?" Next, I give them an *Encouraging* word. Fourth, I *Ask* if there's anything I can pray for them. And last, I try to determine if I *Know* someone they need to know. I've used this tool often to help me engage people for the first time.

The principles of personal engagement apply to all kinds of people. When others make us feel uncomfortable, we need to move *toward* them rather than shying away. (I'm not suggesting we foolishly move toward abusive or violent people. They need another kind of help.) We need to make conscious choices to start conversations with gays, poor people, rich people, and individuals of different political persuasions, ethnic backgrounds and races. Some of us have the hardest time being kind to narrow, rigid, judgmental people—which means we belong in that very category!

Too many Christians value their position on guns, gay marriage, immigration, or any of a dozen other issues more than they value God's command to be an open vessel to carry the love of Christ to a decaying and dark world. When we demand our rights, we lose our voice. We're so intent on taking our stand that we fail to follow the Master in loving the lost and the least, the powerful and the powerless. We're looking for a fight, and they're looking for a fight—that's a bomb with a lit fuse!

Peter Haas is a pastor in Minneapolis and the author of *Pharisectomy: How to Remove Your Inner Pharisee and Other Religiously Transmitted Diseases.*[20] His church is in a community with a large LGBTQ community. A young man came to him and asked bluntly, "I know you're a Christian. What's your position on homosexuality?"

Peter responded, "Let's do this: let's meet six times to get to know each other. At the end of our meetings, you can ask me that question. Would you make a commitment to meet with me six times?"

The man agreed. Over the course of their conversations, they shared their life stories, their hopes, and their dreams. At the end of the sixth meeting, Peter told him, "Okay, you can ask your question now."

The man broke down in tears and said, "I don't need to ask it." The love he felt and the connection he made with Peter told him all he needed to know about Peter's heart. His initial question weeks before was focused on right and wrong, but the warmth of the relationship broke down barriers and built a connection of trust.

If we watch and read the news with a kingdom perspective, we'll find many opportunities to show compassion for people who feel like outcasts. For example, as the threat of terrorism has spread in recent years, some Muslim families in America have reason to wonder if others are suspicious of them, and their kids sometimes feel ostracized at school. An insightful, caring parent can make a special effort to begin or build a relationship with a Muslim mom or dad . . . or anyone else who might feel vulnerable and unwanted.

How do we treat lesbian and gay parents and their kids? Do we warn our kids to stay away, and do we spread gossip about those families? Or do we invite them to come to our kids' parties and let our kids go to theirs? If we reach out to get to know them, to love and accept them as people created in the image of God and of infinite worth, we'll probably raise eyebrows—both among those people who are amazed that we love them, and among plenty of disapproving Christians critical of our reaching out.

The principle of love and engagement applies to anyone or any groups that make us feel uncomfortable. God wants us to move toward them instead of standing back in suspicion. Do we only socialize in places where we find people just like us, where we feel completely safe and accepted? Or do we make a point to go to events where we can rub shoulders with people who are very different from us? What if Jesus had stayed only with the Father and the Spirit in heaven? We'd be in big trouble! He loved us enough to make the ultimate trip from eternity into time, from heaven to earth. Do we love people enough to go to their homes, invite them to ours, sit next to them at events, and have real conversations?

Our influence on others isn't primarily a war of truths. Our goal shouldn't be to out-think and out-argue them so they *have* to agree with us. The greatest impact we have on others is what Peter Haas modeled: loving people so much that their hearts melt. When they're convinced we love them (not just because we've told them, but because they sense the love is authentic and lasting), they'll be more open to listen to our ideas. Love comes first. It's not an afterthought, it's not compromise, and it's not a weakness. Genuine love is essential if we are to follow Jesus' example. Our impact isn't really in our words; it's our attitude, the look in our eyes when we talk to people.

But not all those who make us feel uncomfortable are outcasts. Sometimes we are more irritated with the rich and powerful, the people who believe they have the right to dominate and intimidate anyone who questions them. It's hard to love powerful, defiant people, but Jesus did. He engaged with the Pharisees and Sadducees to show them the Father's love. In fact, much of John's gospel is a running account of Jesus' interactions with the religious elite. He loved them enough to tell them the truth.

I met with a leading figure in the African-American Islamic community, a man who has made the news countless times for his angry, outlandish comments about our country. We spent time talking about the things that matter to each of us, and we enjoyed a meal together. At the end, I prayed for him in Jesus' name. When I finished, he looked at me and smiled, "From this day forward, you will always be my friend." I don't think our interaction changed his mind, but at least we built a bridge of respect so we can have more conversations. That's a start . . . a very good start.

FRIENDS, GROUPS, AND CLASSES

Small groups and classes in the church can multiply the impact of individual believers as they band together to be even saltier and brighter. A group of friends can tackle a large service project, such as volunteering to build a house for Habitat for Humanity or serving a church or orphanage overseas on a mission trip. Or they may get involved in a long-term commitment to tutor children at a local school. One tutor is certainly welcome, but a group of tutors has a multiplied impact—on the children, their parents, and the teachers. Women in a group may mentor single mothers, and sometimes the boyfriends are open to input from mature, godly men. The group can volunteer to serve regularly at a shelter or a center for seniors. The opportunities in every community are almost endless.

When we serve in our communities or overseas, most people don't care what church we attend or the fine points of our theology. They just want to see our hearts and our willingness to roll up our sleeves to pitch in. We often want to put Christian groups and denominations in boxes and label them "acceptable" or "unacceptable" based on our criteria, but this practice divides instead of uniting people who want to show compassion to others. We all just represent Jesus. That's enough, and that's plenty.

OUR CHURCHES

If God has given you a heart to make a difference in your community and you want to marshal your church's people and resources to meet a particular need, don't go to the pastor and demand that he make it happen. Instead, go to him with a humble heart, a vision for effectiveness, and an offer to lead this endeavor.

If you want your church to be more involved in the city, do your homework. A good idea and a demand for the pastor to rearrange his priorities aren't enough. Spend time at the city council meetings, visit the homeless shelter and meet with the director, get involved in the school, or invest your time and resources in the outreach so you know the needs and you have a reasonable plan for the church's involvement.

Even better, first get your group or class to participate, at least for several months. Then, when you go to the pastor, you can show a track record of commitment and involvement. Your experiences will have answered a lot of questions and built bridges of trust. By then the group will be an example and a catalyst for many others to get involved.

Can I make a suggestion? If you approach your pastor with an idea for church ministry or a community outreach, you can make two important assumptions: First, your pastor genuinely wants to meet the needs of people—that's why he became a pastor in the first place. And second, your pastor probably already has plenty on his (or her) plate. All godly leaders live with the tension between wanting to do far more but having limited time and resources. So please don't assume any hesitation is a character flaw in the pastor! Recognize the complexity of leading a volunteer organization like a church, make positive assumptions, and offer to lead or help in any way you can. The people in my church know that if they come to me with an idea and if I feel it's a good one, I will say, "That's a great idea. Go for it! You're in charge!"

There are, though, larger problems that seem overwhelming: signs of cultural drift in abortion, gay marriage, gun violence, racial divides, and immigration, to name a few. We aren't helpless. We are children of the King who invites us to come boldly to his throne of grace to find help in times of need—times like now! Churches can invite their people to pray, to vote, and to speak up about the issues that matter most. We may not be able to entirely stop and reverse the drift in our culture, but God may answer our prayers to at least slow the slide and bring people to the Savior.

THE FATHER'S HEART

Jesus gave us a window on the heart of the Father. In the week before he was killed, he foretold the end of the age, and he painted a picture of salvation and judgment. In the story he tells in Matthew 25:31-46, the king represents God. What matters to him? Not power, not prestige, and not accumulated possessions, but caring for the lost and the least. The king identifies with the most vulnerable in his kingdom, and people who share his heart pour out their love for him in sacrificial service. But his faithful followers were confused. They said, "Lord, when did we see you hungry and feed you, or thirsty and give you something to drink? When did we see you a stranger and invite you in, or needing clothes and clothe you? When did we see you sick or in prison and go to visit you?" The King replied, "Truly I tell you, whatever you did for one of the least of these brothers and sisters of mine, you did for me" (Matt. 25:37–40).

Jesus is saying that the true measure of our understanding of his grace and our devotion to him is compassionate engagement with people who have nothing to offer us in return. God isn't impressed with our grand visions and elaborate programs, and he isn't happy when we invest our lives in secondary things instead of his kingdom's values of kindness, justice, and righteousness. But he's very impressed when we stop our pursuit of selfish agendas, and then become channels of his grace to the disadvantaged around us.

If we're cowards—not salty and hiding our lights—we won't have an impact for Christ on those around us. If we're obnoxious, demanding that people agree with us, we'll certainly have an impact, but not the kind God wants us to have. Being salt and light requires us to be people who have equally radical commitments to love and truth, not one or the other. We love people dearly, listen intently, and patiently get to know them, but we're not afraid to speak up about Jesus and the truth of the Bible. When we do, many will applaud, some will believe, but a few will persecute us. Don't be persecuted for being an angry, defiant, demanding religious Pharisee. But if you're persecuted for loving people the way Jesus loved and speaking the truth the way he spoke it, you're in good company.

THINK ABOUT IT . . .

Remember that Jesus sacrificed to serve you so you have the spiritual resources to sacrifice to serve others.

1. Who makes you feel uncomfortable or angry in your church or community? What would it look like for you to move toward those people? What specific actions will you take? What do you expect—from them and yourself—as you patiently and tenaciously engage them?

2. Do some research to identify some short-term and long-term opportunities to engage people and meet needs in your neighborhood and community. (Look at the list at the end of this chapter for ideas.)

3. What is the most encouraging, inspiring point in this chapter? What concept, story, or command challenges you?

Lord, give me your heart for the lost and the least, and give me the courage to step up and step out to represent you in our community. I want to be salty, and I want your light to shine through me. Fill me with more grace than ever and help me grasp your truth so I can communicate it clearly. Lord, break my heart with what breaks yours.

GO DEEPER . . .

1. What does 1 John 3:1-2 say about your identity in Christ?

2. How does Jer. 29:4-14 describe God's purpose for you?

3. How does 2 Tim. 2:1-10 show you how to stand strong and stay on track?

To prod you to brainstorm short-term and long-term opportunities to be involved in your community, consider contacting some of these agencies. You will probably think of many others as well.

> Tutoring in schools
> Women's shelter
> Men's shelter
> Meals on Wheels
> Helping Hands
> Food pantries
> Pregnancy centers
> Teaching vocational skills
> Seniors
> Refugees

CHAPTER 7

WALKING TOGETHER

If you go out looking for friends, you're going to
find they are very scarce. If you go out to be a
friend, you'll find them everywhere.

—ZIG ZIGLAR

Americans (and all of us in Western culture) live in an individualistic society—probably the most individualistic culture in the history of the world. We value independence, and make heroes of men and women who perform amazing feats in sports, business, or entertainment. In addition, the fabric of family relationships and close communities has been affected by mobility and torn by the frantic pace of modern life. People used to live their whole lives near their parents and grandparents in a community that knew them. Although people are now more connected than ever through social media, those tools don't provide the soul-satisfying depth of relationships people desperately need. We may have hundreds or even thousands of "friends," but we feel lonelier than ever. *TIME* magazine reports that the disconnection in our society affects more than our sense of belonging. Feeling emotionally isolated "could be the next big public-health issue, on par with obesity and substance abuse."[21]

GO TOGETHER

An African proverb says, "If you want to go fast, go alone. If you want to go far, go together." We need to go far to fulfill God's calling in our lives. Christians in America often read the Bible as an individualistic self-help manual and don't see that a vibrant spiritual life can only be experienced in the web of supportive, strong, honest relationships. In the Scriptures we find a wide range of "one another" passages that emphasize the importance of close connections. God wants us to love, forgive, accept, rebuke, bear with, wait for, and confess our sins to one another.

The letter to the Hebrews was written during a time of severe persecution of the Jewish Christians. Other Jews taunted them and told them to give up on Jesus. For many of the Christians, going back to their old faith and practices seemed easier. The writer of this letter told them over and over, "Don't drift away from Christ! He's your true hope. He's the fulfillment of all the promises of the Old Testament. He's the one your ancestors were looking for!" Early in the letter, he warns them:

So watch your step, friends. Make sure there's no evil unbelief lying around that will trip you up and throw you off course, diverting you from the living God. For as long as it's still God's Today, keep each other on your toes so sin doesn't slow down your reflexes. If we can only keep our grip on the sure thing we started out with, we're in this with Christ for the long haul. (Heb. 3:12-14, MSG)

The writer understood that people don't make their most important decisions in a vacuum; they make them in the context of relationships. He knew that if we hang around people who doubt and drift, we're tempted to do the same. But if we spend time with people who are holding tight to Jesus, we'll find the strength to remain strong and stay the course. He encouraged his readers to hold on to one another so they can hold on to Jesus:

Let's keep a firm grip on the promises that keep us going. He always keeps his word. Let's see how inventive we can be in encouraging love and helping out, not avoiding worshiping together as some do but spurring each other on, especially as we see the big Day approaching. (Heb. 10:23-25, MSG)

The writer points people to the ultimate reward of "the Day" when Christ will rule on his throne and will make all things right. In the meantime, we have to encourage each other to hold on to his promises because those promises are sure. We can't take anything for granted. Drift happens even during the good times, and in seasons of difficulty people become discouraged and find excuses to stay away from God and his people. We don't need "happy talk" that lacks substance. We need people who love us enough to speak the truth to us—the truth about our pain and sorrow, the truth about God's greatness and grace, and the truth of his promise that he'll use everything for good if we'll trust him. And then we need to love others with the same intention and intensity.

If we notice someone hasn't been around for a while, we need to show enough love to call and say, "Hey, I haven't seen you lately. I've missed you. Are you doing okay? Can I do anything to help? How can I pray for you?" This kind of initiative may seem intrusive today, but it's necessary if we're going to be deeply involved with each other.

Do we care enough to get involved in people's lives? Do we love them enough to ask a question or two—not to condemn or control, but to offer a hand of love and encouragement?

I would rather walk with a friend in the dark, than alone in the light.

HELEN KELLER

We naturally want to pass on the wisdom we've gained to those we love. But sometimes, the advice we give—and the advice they think they've received—can be both confusing and humorous. Not long ago I asked my son Wilfredo, Jr. to think back on his childhood and tell me what advice I gave that he most remembers. I expected him to instantly relate pearls of wisdom he had learned from me. Instead, he said, "Dad, you must have been impatient with me a lot because you often said, "Son, like Jesus told Judas, 'Whatever you do, do quickly!'" After we both laughed, he smiled and asked, "Dad, I was always a little confused by that. Were you calling me Judas?" And we laughed even more.

GENERATION TO GENERATION

As our society has become instantly and widely connected on the surface but fragmented underneath, the generations have become isolated from each other. Each generation has a unique perspective, passion, and purpose, and we would do well to see the value in one another. Yet instead of appreciating both those who have the wisdom of years *and* those with the idealism of youth, we tend to bond with our own generation and then blame, criticize, and withdraw from the other ones.

Too often, young Millennials (born after 1981) and Boomers (born between 1946 and 1964) view each other in stark and negative stereotypes: Boomers see young people as irresponsible, self-absorbed kids who feel entitled to everything, and young people see older Americans (especially those in their families) as judgmental and boring, with faulty memories.

The generation between Boomers and Millennials is the Busters (born between 1965 and 1980). Experts have identified many distinctions among these three; one of them is how they relate to institutions. Boomers created many of our institutions and hold them as sacred, Millennials are suspicious of institutions, and Busters believe that institutions are significant only when they bring value to people. When it comes to the church, many of the programs were founded by driven, achievement-oriented Boomers; Busters insist on seeing the actual benefits these institutions bring to people; and Millennials either stay away altogether or start their own.[22]

We've come of age in very different worlds, so we can't expect people of different generations to see problems and opportunities through the same lenses. Think of daily communications. Boomers were thrilled to have a rotary phone in their homes, young Busters were the first to use thirty-pound "mobile phones" for business calls when they traveled, and Millennials are constantly connected with the world by the device in their pockets. Boomers value stability and authority, Busters thrive on friendships and want to protect the environment, and Millennials treasure authenticity above all else. We're very different—a fact that often leads to negative and painful assumptions.

Every generation tends to discount the others. One older man believed he had come across a perfect description of young people today: "The counts of the indictment are luxury, bad manners, contempt for authority, disrespect to elders, and love for chatter in place of exercise." But this sentence came from a 1907 essay about how the older Greeks in the Classic Age viewed the young people in their world, centuries before Christ.[23] And we can safely assume the same negative conclusions have been drawn by every subsequent older generation about younger generations.

Today's Millennials aren't breaking this mold; they're following the example of every generation of young people before them. They're learning, growing, and gaining wisdom from experience. Eventually these disrespectful, irresponsible kids become mature adults and run the world. That's what happened in the lives of Busters, Boomers, and the Greatest Generation (who grew up during the Depression and World War II). A little perspective lowers our swords and lets us see the value in people who are significantly younger or older than ourselves.

In our churches, events and classes specifically designed for one segment of the congregation too often separate the generations from one another. These targeted strategies have value, but we need to also have a strategy to bring people together, to learn from and celebrate one another. We need each other's wisdom and insights so all of us can avoid drift and stay on track. Millennials are connected, eager, and idealistic: they need to be unleashed! Boomers are available, long for a compelling purpose, and have more resources than any generation in history. Busters can be an important bridge between these two groups, but they're too often overwhelmed caring for both their teenagers and their aging parents. If we work together, God will use us to do incredible things for his kingdom.

God gives us our relatives—thank God we can choose our friends.

—ETHEL WATTS MUMFORD

FRIENDS AND MENTORS

People simply don't thrive without at least a few good friends. We don't need a hundred, but we need at least two or three people we allow to see the best and the worst in us. How do we know who are our true friends? They are the ones who don't envy us when we succeed, and they don't despise us when we fail. A proverb tells us, "A friend loves at all times, and a brother is born for a time of adversity" (Prov. 17:17). We hope a brother (or sister) will stay with us when times are hard, but a true friend loves us at all times—and all kinds of times.

Author and pastor Tim Keller comments, "A friend always lets you in and never lets you down." He identifies four traits of friendship:

- Constancy—Friends don't drift away (or run away) when times are hard. If anything, they're more involved in helping us handle the difficulties.

- Carefulness—Friends are perceptive and sensitive. They notice what's going on inside us, ask delicate questions, and speak with diplomacy and tact.

- Candor—Friends aren't so careful that they avoid saying the hard things we need to hear. They aren't bullies, but they aren't cowards, either.

- Counsel—We can trust friends with our highest hopes and our deepest secrets. We can share our pain without fear that we'll be laughed at or be given a quick fix to a complicated problem. And we can share our joys without fear that our success threatens the relationship.[24]

These are the friends all of us want but few have. They embody the two traits Jesus came to give: grace (constancy and carefulness) and truth (candor and counsel). Our first step, then, is to *be* this kind of friend. Not everyone wants this level of vulnerability and commitment, but when it happens, it's beautiful and powerful.   Mentors combine the strong traits of friendship with a teaching and modeling role in another person's life. Friends are peers, but mentors take responsibility to coach, model, open doors, give advice, and be the chief cheerleader for the person they help grow. We can find mentors in any kind of organization: in business, the church, non-profits, or clubs. We see the impact of mentors in the Scriptures when we look at the powerful relationship of Barnabas and Paul, Paul and Timothy, Moses and Joshua, and Elijah and Elisha.

No matter how long we look, we may not find two people as different as Elijah and Elisha. Elijah, the older man, lived in the wilderness and looked like John the Baptist, wearing a hairy garment and a leather belt around his waist (2 Kings 1:8).

He was intense and laser focused on doing God's will, a prophet of prophets. Elisha lived in a house and probably looked like an accountant. His head was shaved and smooth, and he wore regular clothes instead of a sheepskin mantle. On a street corner, we might not pick him out of a crowd of two.

Elisha was fascinated with Elijah's faith and spiritual power, but Elijah always wanted his protégé to count the cost. They traveled to several regions: Gilgal, Bethel, and Jericho. At each place, the older man told Elisha to stay. It wasn't that Elijah was annoyed; he was asking Elisha to stop and consider his choices: Would the cost of following God be too high? At each point, would it be easier to stop and go no farther? Elijah knew that radical obedience is always hard: it inevitably takes you places you would never choose to go. In his wisdom and courtesy, he invited his protégé to reflect carefully before taking the next step. Each time, Elisha chose to follow. He wanted to stay as close as he could.

Their final stop was on the other side of the Jordan River. To get there, Elijah rolled up his cloak and struck the water with it. The waters of the Jordan parted and allowed the two men to cross on dry ground. Elijah knew his time was short, and he asked Elisha, "Tell me, what can I do for you before I am taken from you?" Elisha asked for a double portion of his spirit (2 Kings 2:9).

Elijah's prophetic ministry had begun with a miracle of judgment (1 Kings 17:1), and it ended with the miracle of God taking him to heaven in "a chariot of fire" and a whirlwind. Elisha, now alone, returned with the cloak that had fallen from Elijah's shoulders. When he got back to the Jordan River, he struck the water with it. Instantly, the water parted and Elisha walked to the other side. It was a miracle exactly like the one Elisha had seen God perform through Elijah (2 Kings 2:11-14).

Elisha's next miracle also involved water. The men of Jericho came to him and complained, "Look, our lord, this town is well situated, as you can see, but the water is bad and the land is unproductive." Elisha told them to bring him a bowl, and he instructed them to put salt in it. He took the salt to the city springs and threw it into the water. He announced, "This is what the LORD says: 'I have healed this water. Never again will it cause death or make the land unproductive.'" From that day, the water from the spring remained pure and refreshing (2 Kings 2:19-22).

Water is a metaphor for our relationships—in our families, our neighborhoods, and at work. Like water, Christians are to be sweet, nourishing, life-giving. This water also symbolizes the church's influence in our communities. The gospel of grace through Jesus Christ is attractive, reasonable, clear, and life changing. And don't miss the important paradox in this story: the water of Jericho became sweet only after salt was poured into it. Similarly, the only way for us to become sweet to those around us is to be salty.

When we begin to drift, we naturally begin to accommodate cultural shifts, angrily oppose them, or give up in withdrawal. We need a mentor like Elijah who will show us what it means to live for God in a corrupt society, and we need a mentor like Elisha who shows us how saltiness produces sweetness—in us and in those who come into contact with us.

The rest of the story is that God did, indeed, give Elisha a double portion of Elijah's spirit. Elisha's success came from the power of their relationship, and he performed twice as many miracles as his mentor. Both of these men were intentional: one had something to give, and the other wanted desperately to receive. They had many obstacles to overcome, including their stark differences in background, clothing, and appearance. But that didn't matter to either of them. They had a bigger purpose than fitting into anyone's narrow expectations. Their relationship was rooted in the calling of God, and they were committed to each other.

Have you ever had a mentor who poured his or her wisdom into you? Have you been a mentor to anyone for a season? Both roles demand a price in time and effort, and when a mentor pushes a protégé to greater depths of humility or heights of accomplishment, the friction can throw off sparks! Still, the pattern of Scripture and the testimony of believers through the ages is that a mentor can make all the difference in a person's growth. Elisha's ministry not only included twice as many miracles, it also lasted almost five times longer.

Friendship is unnecessary, like philosophy, like art. . . . It has no survival value; rather it is one of those things which give value to survival.

—C.S. LEWIS

God has put some wonderful people in my life who have been friends and mentors. When I became a Christian at fourteen, I met Efrain. He was only fifteen, but he was instrumental in the earliest years of my walk of faith. We've been close friends and brothers for over thirty-five years. He's actually more than a friend; he's family. He is my brother-in-law, married to my wife's sister. He has been with me since the beginning of my ministry here at New Life Covenant, and he serves as the Executive Pastor. He has been a confidant I can trust with my life. When

I've gone through difficulties, I've leaned on him for comfort and support. When I've faced difficult choices, I've trusted him to ask the right questions, help me process the options, and clarify the Lord's guidance. Even today, I know many wonderful Christian leaders, but I still go to Efrain because we have a history together. He knows me, and he has seen how God has led me in the past. I trust that he wants the best for me. He always communicates God's grace to me, and he never hesitates to speak God's truth to my heart. He has seen me at my best, and he's never jealous. He has seen me at my worst, and he never laughs or leaves.

My wife Elizabeth is my most trusted companion, but in the early years of our marriage, I didn't think we'd make it. We were both believers, but that fact was no guarantee of smooth sailing. We butted heads, and we butted hard! The first five years of our marriage were more like wandering in the desert than living in the Promised Land. We were serving the Lord, but we really didn't like each other.

Finally, we both came to a point of brokenness. We couldn't make life work on our own, so we cried out to God. Gradually, hurts were healed, communication became more positive, and trust replaced resentment. God performed radical heart surgery on both of us, and we've become each other's biggest cheerleaders. We're partners in our marriage, as parents, and in ministry. She speaks God's love and truth into my life, and I welcome her input. She warns me when she senses I'm drifting into pride or anger, and she gently brings me back to the grace and purposes of God.

We simply can't stay on course (or get back on course) without the loving, wise, bold input of people who care enough about us to tell the truth. Let me make these suggestions:

- *Evaluate the impact of your friendships.* Who are the people who point you to the Lord, and who are those who distract or discourage you? Be honest. It's very hard to admit that someone we've trusted for years may not be a good influence on us. And it may be even harder to realize we've had a negative impact on those who are closest to us.

- *Be a better friend.* Ask God to put a few people on your heart and provide you with wisdom to be the best friend you can be. Share your heart at one level deeper than you have before with these people. Your honesty will be an invitation for them to reciprocate. Don't offer quick answers to complex problems. Instead, ask good questions and listen . . . really listen. How do you know if you're listening? One way is to ask second and third questions instead of thinking about how you're going to solve the other person's problem or give "the right answer." A true friend facilitates self-discovery and personal responsibility. As communication deepens and trust grows, the friendship will become stronger.

- *Look for a genuine partner.* God may bless you with several friends who are true soul mates, but ask him for at least one person who "sticks closer than a brother." The Lone Ranger needed Tonto; Batman needed Robin; the Cisco Kid needed Pancho. ("Oh, Pancho!") All of us need someone who has our back no matter what. Your spouse may be that person. If not, hopefully God will produce that kind of relationship between you.

- *Find a mentor.* Even better, find *the right* mentor. Early in my calling, I looked for someone to step into my life to train me. I asked several Christian leaders to play that role in my life, but perhaps they didn't see much potential, or maybe they thought it would be too much work to turn me into an effective man of God. Whatever the reason, it took a while for me to find someone to be my life coach, yet over the years, God has led me to some gifted, wise, and godly men who were willing to pour everything they knew into me. I'll never forget them.

- *Sooner or later, become a mentor to someone.* If you're a leader, you already have opportunities to mentor people who report to you. Don't use them as stepping-stones to get to your destination. Value them, believe in them, ask God for a vision of their future, and then speak to them with love and boldness about what you believe God has for them.

- *Choose wisely.* We need to trust God to show us how to shrewdly invest our time and our hearts. We can become open channels for mentors to pour their wisdom and skills into us, and then we can pour what we have learned into others. As Timothy's mentor, Paul explained the flow from one generation to the next: "You then, my son, be strong in the grace that is in Christ Jesus. And the things you have heard me say in the presence of many witnesses entrust to reliable people who will also be qualified to teach others" (2 Tim. 2:1-2). Paul was Timothy's mentor, Timothy became a mentor to "reliable people," and then those people became teachers and leaders to others. Today, all of us are the recipients of love and wisdom passed down through generations of spiritual mentors.

Our friends usually share a long history with us. We feel comfortable discussing our hopes and fears without wondering if they'll walk out. However, the relationships we have with mentors are usually more structured and purposeful than those with friends. We ask a leader to be a mentor so we can learn particular lessons and gain specific skills, usually for a limited time. Both friends and mentors, however, are essential if we are going to avoid drift and boldly engage the people and issues in our culture.

The process is reversed in these two vital relationships: Be a friend first, and then find a friend. Find a mentor first, and then become a mentor. These relationships are part of "walking together."

If you've read this chapter with a sense of discouragement because you've tried to find friends and a mentor but you haven't been successful, don't give up. I've gone through very dry times when I felt alone, and worse, I felt misunderstood and abandoned. I could have given up, but I sensed God whispering to me to keep trusting him to give me people who would walk with me. He has done exactly that, and I'm sure he'll do the same for you. Don't give up. God is faithful.

THINK ABOUT IT . . .

Remember that God wants us to walk together with friends and mentors. With them, we'll stay the course; without them, we'll almost certainly drift.

1. Do you agree or disagree with the African proverb: "If you want to go fast, go alone. If you want to go far, go together"? Explain your answer.

2. Who are you walking with? What kind of impact are you having on your friends? What impact are they having on you? Do you need to make any changes? If so, what are they?

3. If you've ever had a mentor, what influence did that person have on your life and your career? If you haven't had a mentor, what benefits could you gain from choosing the right person and learning from him or her?

Lord Jesus, even you didn't walk alone. You had three—Peter, James, and John—who were your closest friends, as well as the other disciples and the women who followed you. Help me be a great friend, and help me choose the right people to pour my life into.

GO DEEPER . . .

1. What does 2 Cor. 5:17-21 say about your identity in Christ?

2. How does Titus 2:11-15 describe God's purpose for you?

3. How does Heb. 12:1-3 show you how to stand strong and stay on track?

CHAPTER 8

NO EXCUSES

Success is not final, failure is not fatal:
it is the courage to continue that counts.

—WINSTON CHURCHILL

Staying the course in a shifting culture is very hard. It's much easier to just get along, to fight back in anger, or to give up. When life is hard, many people bail out on their marriages, their children, their integrity, their commitments, and even on God. A moment of drift that isn't noticed and corrected can quickly become a more significant slide. White lies have to be covered up with additional and bigger deceptions. Any choice to avoid the hard work of communicating with a spouse, kids, or an employer is a brick in a wall that becomes a fortress to keep people out.

Many Christians in our country confuse the American dream with the kingdom of God, but God never promised believers an easy, smooth life with fabulous riches. Scripture makes it clear that if we walk with Christ, we'll suffer, yet if we trust him, our suffering will produce perseverance, a godly character, and a hope built on the foundation of God's love, strength, and purposes (Rom. 5:3-5).

If we treasure success, pleasure, and approval more than God and his kingdom, we'll make excuses for our failures, and we'll blame others for our problems. I don't intend to be mean, but many Christians in our country have a shallow and weak faith that collapses under pressure—including the unavoidable pressure of being a flawed person living in a flawed and fallen world.

THE TEST OF GROWTH

I believe significant spiritual growth occurs only through difficulties. The Scriptures show us how God wants to use heartaches—whatever the cause—to humble us, deepen our faith, and shape our character.

In Genesis, we read that Joseph had been a self-centered favorite son. His brothers betrayed him and sold him into slavery in Egypt. His Egyptian master falsely accused him of sexual indiscretion, and he was thrown into prison for about twenty years. In prison he impressed and benefited a fellow inmate who promptly forgot to repay the favor upon his release. It appeared that Joseph had hit a dead end, but God used those experiences to strengthen his faith, not destroy it. God humbles the proud and exalts the humble, and a humbled Joseph was raised from the depths of the prison to become Prime Minister of the most powerful nation on earth. In that role, God used him to save the lives of millions from famine, including his father and brothers who had long ago lost hope that he was still alive (Gen. 37; 39-47).

Later, after their father died, the brothers were afraid Joseph would take revenge for their betrayal so long before. Yet with amazing faith in the sovereignty and goodness of God, Joseph explained, "Don't be afraid. Am I in the place of God? You intended to harm me, but God intended it for good to accomplish what is now being done, the saving of many lives. So then, don't be afraid. I will provide for you and your children" (Gen. 50:19-21).

Joseph wasn't looking for an opportunity for payback. Instead, the long years of suffering had taught him that God's ways are far different from ours. He asked his fearful brothers the rhetorical question: "Am I in the place of God?" In other words, "Who am I to assume that I know more than God about ruling the universe? Why are my desires and my comfort more important than his perfect will?" Because Joseph trusted God's wisdom and provision, he could make the honest statement: "You meant to harm me, but God used even your betrayal and many years of slavery and imprisonment for his good purposes." Joseph's deep faith eliminated any attempted justification to be bitter and take revenge. His faith enabled him to see his situation from God's perspective and stay the course.

The story of Job is one of the most painful in the Bible. He never understood why God allowed him to suffer such tragic losses and health problems. When he prayed, it seemed the heavens were closed and God was completely absent. Still, he trusted that God would use his suffering for good—he didn't know how, when, or why, but he still trusted God. He told the men who claimed to know all the answers:

"But if I go to the east, he is not there;
     if I go to the west, I do not find him.

When he is at work in the north, I do not see him;
   when he turns to the south, I catch no glimpse
   of him.
But he knows the way that I take;
   when he has tested me, I will come forth as gold."
   (Job 23:8-10)

FIRE, SHEARS, AND A POTTER'S WHEEL

The Bible uses three powerful metaphors to describe the way God shapes our lives through suffering: refining precious metals through fire, pruning healthy plants, and shaping clay pots. The common theme in each instance is that the raw material doesn't call the shots; the master craftsman or gardener is in control. When gold or silver is refined, the ore is put into a blazing furnace where the metal melts and separates from the other materials. Without the heat, the precious metal would remain hidden and useless. In the same way, God uses the heat of heartaches to burn away our impure motives and selfish behaviors so we want him and his will more than ever before.

On the night he was betrayed, Jesus walked with his disciples in a vineyard. He used the moment to explain a vital truth of spiritual growth: "I am the true vine, and my Father is the gardener. He cuts off every branch in me that bears no fruit, while every branch that does bear fruit he prunes so that it will be even more fruitful" (John 15:1-2).

We might think gardeners only get rid of dead or diseased plants, but that's not the case in growing grapes. In a vineyard, the master gardener prunes healthy plants so they will grow even stronger and bear even more fruit. Quite often, the pruning is severe; the gardener leaves only stumps. To the untrained eye, this degree of pruning looks unnecessary, even foolish, but it is the way grapevines produce an abundance of delicious fruit.

Christians are often confused about the reason for their suffering: Is it the natural consequence of sin, or is it God pruning a healthy, growing plant so it bears more fruit? Two tests help us determine the difference. First, if we're knowingly and willingly violating the clear commands of God described in the Bible, it's sin. If, however, we truly attempt to honor God but still encounter setbacks, it's probably pruning. Second, we can solicit feedback from wise believers. We need to talk to mature Christians who understand the difference between the consequences of sin and God's skillful pruning. Look for someone who has a track record of discerning the difference in his or her life.

Many Christians are shocked when they suffer hardships. They believe their devotion to God has earned them God's blessings, but obedience doesn't entitle us to an easy life. Instead, obedience shows God we're completely his, and as a master gardener, he prunes us so we'll be more fruitful in our relationships and service.

God is too good to be unkind.
He is too wise to be confused.
If I cannot trace His hand,
I can always trust His heart.
—CHARLES SPURGEON

The third metaphor is a potter working with malleable clay. During a time of national calamity, the prophet Isaiah cried out to God:

Yet you, Lord, are our Father.
We are the clay, you are the potter;
we are all the work of your hand. (Isa. 64:8)

To prepare for a sermon on the potter and the clay, I took a course from a potter. I learned a lot by getting my hands dirty. I had to get the consistency of the clay just right, and I had to put it in exactly the right place on the wheel. Then, with wet and flexible hands, I gradually formed a pot. (Actually, I made a lot of mistakes and had to start over again many times, but I understood the point that the potter is in complete control.) I asked the professional to come on the stage and shape a pot during the sermon. Not once, I explained, did the clay refuse to respond to his touch. It didn't talk back, and it didn't complain. It never questioned, "What are you doing? I have a better idea for a pot." God designed us to be containers for his presence, his anointing, and his purposes. But we don't hold those blessings for our sake. God has a higher purpose for his pots.

Every time that God puts us (or allows us to be) in the fire, under the pruning shears, or on the potter's wheel, we have a choice to accept the experience as part of his eternal design for us, or to resist and walk away. Humanity's default reaction is to complain and blame others for our problem.

When God confronted Adam for his sin in the Garden, he blamed Eve, and he blamed God for bringing her to him (Gen. 3:11-12). When Saul faced Samuel's rebuke for disobedience, he blamed his soldiers for sparing animals and the enemy king (1 Sam. 15:13-35). When Jesus asked a man who had been crippled for thirty-eight years if he wanted to get well, rather than saying "yes" or "no" the man immediately began to complain that he had no one to help him get into the pool (John 5:1-15). In Jesus' famous parable about a rich man who left his investments in the hands of three servants, two of them saw multiplied gains, but the third was fearful and made excuses for hiding his part in the ground. When the owner came back, he didn't buy the servant's excuses. He told him, "You wicked, lazy servant! So you knew that I harvest where I have not sown and gather where I have not scattered seed? Well then, you should have put my money on deposit with the bankers, so that when I returned I would have received it back with interest" (Matt. 25:26-27). The owner took the investment away from the coward and gave it to one who was bold and faithful. Excuses don't cut it with God.

The people who threw palm branches in front of Jesus on Palm Sunday were proclaiming him as the reigning king! They were sure their prayers were answered: Jesus was going to overthrow the Romans and restore Israel's independence. But he deeply disappointed them. He was a king all right, but a very different King from what they expected. A few days later, they shouted, "Crucify him!"

The crowds weren't alone in their disappointment. The disciples had spent over three years with Jesus. They saw him heal the sick, cure lepers, and restore sight to the blind, and they heard him teach with such authority that people were amazed. They had been on his leadership team, sent out to heal the sick and cast out demons! Yet Judas was so disappointed in Jesus that he betrayed him to the Pharisees. And Peter was so frightened that he denied even knowing Jesus. All the rest, except John, ran for their lives. Still, Jesus didn't give up on them. After his resurrection, he came through locked doors to appear to them and reassure them. He spent time with Peter specifically, to assure him of his forgiveness and purpose for his life.

The point is that all of us are sometimes tempted to quit on Jesus. It's easy to conclude that Jesus isn't who we thought he was. Sometimes we are deeply disappointed that he doesn't come through like we want him to. We all drift away from time to time, but we need to have sensitive hearts that respond to God's invitation to come back.

A RIGHT OR A GIFT?

As I talk to believers, I find that many of them have an erroneous view of suffering. If life is hard, they think they've missed God's will. They assume God's calling is always to a pleasant, productive life. If they're in the middle of God's will, they're sure, the sky opens, the birds sing, and everything should be rosy. This incorrect perspective is often combined with a belief they can earn God's blessings: if they've tried at all to go to church, give money, serve, or quit some bad behavior, they feel God owes them a life of uninterrupted blessings. No wonder they cave in when they experience hard times.

Our culture—including all its generations: Boomers, Busters, and Millennials—may be the first in history that hasn't experienced suffering as a normal part of life. If we read the New Testament, we see that first-century Christians *expected* suffering and persecution. The letters of Paul and Peter take it for granted that believers will go through hard times, and they encourage us to cling to God at every moment. And if we say we follow Christ and want to be like him, how can we imagine that we will escape at least a small part of the suffering he experienced?

In the early church, Christians were despised and persecuted by both Romans and unbelieving Jews. Believers sometimes had to run for their lives to escape death. In 64 A.D., the Emperor Nero set Rome on fire. He blamed the Christians and made a public spectacle of punishing some of them by covering them with pitch and setting them on fire to light his balcony. In contrast, today's "suffering" of most Christians in America is far less intense. So rather than reacting to difficulties and challenges with complaints and self-pity, a far better response is to be deeply grateful for all God has given us.

God's blessings are gifts to be enjoyed, not rights we can demand. Everything we find in our hands has been provided by our wise heavenly Father. Some might argue, "I work hard for the money I make." Yes, but who gave you the talents, intelligence, strength, and opportunities to work? Those are God's gifts, too.

We respond to gifts differently than we do rights. We sometimes *demand* our rights (as citizens, YMCA members, defendants in a lawsuit, or whatever) because they are things we feel we deserve. Yet in our relationship with God, the only thing we genuinely deserve is hell. All of us have sinned and fallen short of the glory of God, and the wages of our sin is death (Rom. 3:23; 6:23). We're not entitled to demand *anything*, so everything we experience that's better than hell is a gift from the hand of God. We learn to hold those gifts lightly as our hearts focus more on the giver than the gifts themselves.

This perspective changes how we relate to God, how we use our possessions, and how we treat other people. For instance, my children aren't annoyances I need to control to make my life easier. They are God's treasures and his gifts to me. My role is to cherish them, to develop them, and to launch them so they can serve effectively in God's kingdom.

If we see our possessions, our positions, and popularity as a right, we'll be defensive when anyone challenges us and depressed or angry (or both) when anything is taken from us. And no amount of wealth, comfort, or popularity will satisfy for more than a moment. They can't. God has made us so that only he can truly fill the hole in our souls.

I'm not saying possessions, positions, and popularity are inherently wrong. If we see them as gifts, we can enjoy them without the poison of pride. In 2013, *TIME* magazine named me as one of their "100 Most Influential People" out of seven billion on the planet. My first reaction was utter, complete shock. I had no hint they would consider me for such an honor. Veronica, my assistant, came into my office and said, "Pastor, congratulations!"

I responded, "Thanks. For what?"

She told me about the magazine's selection, but she realized I didn't understand the significance. She blurted out, "Pastor, this is really big!"

It took me a while to realize what the honor meant, but I soon understood that the selection was a gift from God. Suddenly I had a bigger platform to talk about him, and I needed to be a good steward of the opportunity. I wasn't a different husband, father, pastor, or leader on the day the magazine hit the shelves. I was the same person, but God had given me a new door—a door to the world—to walk through to honor him. It was about him, not me.

We looked previously at the parable about the rich man leaving his investments to the three servants. That parable reveals another important principle of the kingdom of God: when we're faithful with a little, God entrusts more to us. When we trust God and please him in obscurity, God often opens doors for us to serve him in a wider world. In response, we're grateful, not arrogant. We realize God has given us the talents and the opportunities each step of the way. At every point of growth in our church, we give God all the glory.

A THREAT AND A PROMISE

The cross was no surprise to Jesus. Time and again, he predicted he would die for the sins of the world. To Peter, it was unthinkable that the King of kings, God's Messiah, would die a criminal's death. When he tried to convince Jesus his predictions certainly were ludicrous, I can imagine he was speaking for all the disciples. Jesus told Peter he had come to the wrong conclusion, and then he explained the essence of what it means to follow him:

> "Whoever wants to be my disciple must deny themselves and take up their cross and follow me. For whoever wants to save their life will lose it, but whoever loses their life for me will find it. What good will it be for someone to gain the whole world, yet forfeit their soul? Or what can anyone give in exchange for their soul?" (Matt. 16:24-26)

Following Jesus is, at the same time, the most challenging and most satisfying life anyone can live. No other life comes close. A person can be the richest, most handsome or beautiful, and have grand titles—he or she can "gain the whole world"—but it all means nothing compared to the wonder of God's love, grace, power, and purposes.

When a train goes through a tunnel and it's dark, you don't throw away the ticket and jump off. You sit still and trust the engineer.

—CORRIE TEN BOOM

Only seven days after the devastating 2010 earthquake in Haiti, a team from our church landed in Santo Domingo and drove a bus full of food and supplies to the people in the destruction zone. We arrived at night, and immediately the bus was surrounded by people who hadn't eaten and had gone without clean water since the moment the ground began shaking. They were terrified and desperate. When we saw the look in their eyes, we wondered if they were going to attack us to get the food. An American with wide eyes came over to me and frantically said, "I think we need to call the Army to come here and distribute the supplies to the people. It's too dangerous for us!"

I told him flatly, "I came here to die. When I left Chicago, I told Elizabeth that I didn't know what to expect when we got here. I explained that we were going to face disease and death—maybe our own." He looked stunned. I repeated the point: "My friend, I came here to serve God and the people affected by this disaster. Did you think you were going to a resort? I came here to give myself totally. I came here to die." I realized my statement sounded a bit dramatic—but I meant every word. To reassure him, I then smiled and said, "Let's help these people."

By this time, the crowd outside the bus was getting rowdy. Many of the people in the bus were frightened. In the thick darkness of night, I got out of the bus and walked into the mass of humanity. I told them we would give them everything we have, but we needed to distribute it in an orderly way. They reluctantly stopped pushing each other, and we handed out our supplies.

Jesus didn't come to earth for a vacation. He came to die. When we follow him, we choose to die, too. In America, sacrifice is almost a dirty word, but in the kingdom of God, it's essential. Too many of us are "consumer Christians" who expect to choose what we like and discard what we don't like about following Jesus. It's like shopping at the grocery store: I'll take this, but no, I don't want that. That's not true discipleship. In reality, following Jesus is a constant "no" to our selfish desires and a constant "yes" to be completely his and do whatever he calls us to do.

When we hold too tightly to anything that doesn't have eternal value, our hands can't receive the things that matter most. When God puts resources and opportunities in our hands, and we give them away in glad service, God gives us even more.

As a wise and loving parent, God doesn't give us everything we want, but he always gives us everything we need to live the abundant life—including enough difficulties to show us our dependence on him. The awe of God's gift of grace shatters our self-righteousness (when we think our own efforts have deserved God's blessing) and obliterates self-pity (when we're disappointed that God hasn't given us all we expected). As we see God's blessings pass through our hands to help hurting people all around us, a sense of wonder fills us with thankfulness and a heartfelt desire to please him in all we say and do.

The cycle of blessing is that we receive from God, we give to others, and God provides more for us to give. And the cycle continues. This is a fundamental principle of the kingdom, the concept of sowing and reaping: We reap *what* we sow, we reap *after* we sow, and we reap *more than* we sow.

THE TRANSFORMING POWER OF GRACE

Some people misunderstand the meaning of grace. They see it as a ticket to do whatever they want, without correction or consequences. They use it as an excuse for disobedience. Grace frees, but it also compels. Dietrich Bonhoeffer was a pastor in Nazi Germany. He stood up for Christ when many in the churches either cowered in fear of Hitler or embraced him as the national savior. Bonhoeffer was under no illusions about the price of following Jesus. In his book, *The Cost of Discipleship*, he described the difference between anemic "cheap grace" and the life-changing power of "costly grace." He wrote:

> Cheap grace is the grace we bestow on ourselves. Cheap grace is the preaching of forgiveness without requiring repentance, baptism without church discipline, Communion without confession. . . . Cheap grace is grace without discipleship, grace without the cross, grace without Jesus Christ, living and incarnate. . . . Costly grace is the treasure hidden in the field; for the sake of it a man will gladly go and sell all that he has. It is the pearl of great price to buy which the merchant will sell all his goods. It is the kingly rule of Christ, for whose sake a man will pluck out the eye which causes him to stumble, it is the call of Jesus Christ at which the disciple leaves his nets and follows him.[25]

In his second letter to the Corinthians, Paul explained the drive produced by grace: "For Christ's love compels us, because we are convinced that one died for all, and therefore all died. And he died for all, that those who live should no longer live for themselves but for him who died for them and was raised again" (2 Cor. 5:14-15). Grace is the motivation for us to die to our selfishness and live radical lives of obedience to our Creator, King, and Savior. Let the grace of God change you from the inside out so that you avoid drift and engage the people around you.

Each of us is a "masterpiece" of God (Eph. 2:10, NLT), and his unconditional love and forgiveness propel us to fulfill the unique purpose he has for us. God's purpose is seldom clear from the beginning. More often, it unfolds as we walk with God, dive into opportunities, and learn from our mistakes and successes. Slowly, the Spirit unveils God's purpose for us. Even then, God may change our direction several times during our lives—not to make us more comfortable, but to make us more useful. Along the way, we may suffer the death of a dream from time to time. Again, we shouldn't be surprised: God is using the fire, the pruning shears, and the potter's wheel to shape us. At every step, we hold more tightly to God than to our concept of his calling. His leading may change our direction, but he never fails.

GOD'S LEADING

Some people are paralyzed because they're aren't sure of God's leading about a particular choice: a house or apartment, a job, a dating relationship, or something else that seems like the most important thing in the world at the moment. We need to keep our minds and hearts riveted on Jesus and his kingdom. We live for him wherever we reside, wherever we work, and whomever we're with at the moment. God is a sovereign, loving Father. He won't always tell us every little choice to make, but we can be sure that if we want to honor him, he'll lead us. Even if we make a mistake, he promises to use it for good in our lives.

Today, I hear a lot of "super-spiritual" talk among believers. It seems like some people want to wear a badge of honor and superiority when they proclaim, "God told me" this or that. I certainly believe God speaks to his children. God spoke and the universe was created, and Jesus is called "the Word," which means it's his nature to communicate with us. But I believe God speaks primarily through the truth of the Scriptures. The vast majority of the will of God is in his Word. Our first priority is to master the law and love, the commandments and the grace found in the Bible.

The claim of hearing God's voice can create tension and misunderstanding in the church. People come to me all the time, supposedly to get some advice or to get a blessing (which often involves them changing churches), and they often begin by saying, "Pastor, God told me . . ." At that point, I've become obsolete: if God has spoken to them, why do they want my input? I call this the "spiritual trump card." What am I supposed to say after that? Sometimes, those who say God has given them particular directions may use this to limit their availability to serve because "God told me to do this, not that." And others don't move at all because God hasn't spoken to them to give specific instructions. But following Jesus isn't about narrowing the options to serve; it's about being willing to touch lives in every possible way.

I'm afraid some people mistake their own desires (or maybe indigestion) for the voice of God. Yes, the Spirit of God whispers and shouts, but his message is often to apply a passage of Scripture and to obey the written Word of the Lord. We need to be very careful to avoid the sin of pride by claiming a special channel to God. I appreciate those who tell me how God has spoken to them through a passage from the Bible, and those who only rarely claim to have heard special directions. Even then, I look for humility. I expect them to say, "It seems God is telling me . . ." instead of "God spoke to me . . ."

Our primary responsibility is to sink our roots deep into God's power and love. Building a relationship with anyone takes time, attention, and heart. Building a relationship with the omnipotent, omniscient, and omnipresent God of glory stretches us to the limit, but it's worth it. Today the "average church attender" goes to church 1.5 times a month, and we can suspect those people aren't involved in small groups or classes, or digging into the Scriptures on their own. This level of interest and involvement leaves them vulnerable to inevitable difficulties they will experience (some of which would probably be avoided if their perceptions were sharpened by a strong relationship with God).

People—even those who *are* involved in church—often try to fill their souls with things that don't satisfy. Only a strong relationship with the almighty, compassionate God can fill the gaping hole in our hearts. God's leading, then, isn't just about accomplishments or even service; he calls us first to himself.

LIFE WORTH LIVING

A heart that is determined to be fully God's doesn't look for excuses, and it doesn't look for someone to blame when life is hard. Instead, it stays focused on God at all times, thanking him for blessings because we realize his gifts are always evidence of his grace, and thanking him for difficulties because we're convinced he is using those for his good purposes.

With that in mind, let's face any challenge and take every opportunity to demonstrate the love of God to the people around us. The problems in our families, our neighborhoods, our nation, and our world often look too big, too deep, and too difficult, but let's choose to engage anyway. Let's imitate Jesus and move toward the hurting with compassion, into decay with the salt of hope, and into darkness with the light of God's truth.

This is the only life worth living. We bask in the love, forgiveness, and acceptance of God, and we offer ourselves as glad sacrifices to him. The closer we get to Christ, the more like him we become.

We are not meant to die merely in order to be dead. God could not want that for the creatures to whom He has given the breath of life. We die in order to live.

—ELISABETH ELLIOT

In his letter to the Philippians, Paul explained that a vital relationship with Jesus radically transforms our source of security, our heart's motivations, and our actions:

> If you've gotten anything at all out of following Christ, if his love has made any difference in your life, if being in a community of the Spirit means anything to you, if you have a heart, if you care—then do me a favor: Agree with each other, love each other, be deep-spirited friends. Don't push your way to the front; don't sweet-talk your way to the top. Put yourself aside, and help others get ahead. Don't be obsessed with getting your own advantage. Forget yourselves long enough to lend a helping hand. Think of yourselves the way Christ Jesus thought of himself. (Phil. 2:1-5, MSG)

The more we experience the reality of Jesus, the more fully invested we become in him and his cause. Half-heartedness won't cut it, and half measures won't do. Our passion is to know him and honor him in every possible way. From the time our eyes open in the morning until they shut at night, we are fully his. We can expect to experience both suffering and blessing, as Jesus did, but through it all we are assured God is present. He is the sovereign king, even when everything appears to be out of control; and he loves us dearly, even when we encounter heartaches.

Many of us mistakenly assume that God's peace means the *absence* of difficulties, but God hasn't given us such assurance. Instead, he promises a sense of his presence *in the midst of* difficulties. The world may be coming apart around us, and those who oppose us may be fierce, but we can stand firm on the stable, secure Rock.

When we obey God out of hearts filled and overflowing with gratitude, we get the greatest blessing of all: the warmth of his love. Jesus assures us, "Whoever has my commands and keeps them is the one who loves me. The one who loves me will be loved by my Father, and I too will love them and show myself to them" (John 14:21). As we follow him, we'll sense his love and power more than ever, and he'll let us into his heart. This is the ultimate blessing, one that can never be taken away.

All the people of great faith I've ever met had two characteristics: kindness and strength. Over years of pursuing God, they've experienced God's warmth and affection. And through the ups and downs of those years, they developed a burning desire to know him and serve him. Their depth of faith didn't come from a single choice; it was the product of countless decisions to choose God instead of what came easy. Their pattern of choices created a habit of the heart to pursue hard after God, no matter what the circumstances, no matter what the risks, no matter where he might lead.

As we develop this habit, we'll go deeper into his love and purposes. We'll enjoy more blessings than we ever imagined, and we'll endure more heartache because we'll identify with the suffering of those around us. More than ever, we'll realize how much we need God. We'll be in deep water of loving the unlovely, serving without acclaim, and putting our lives on the line for people who may not care at all. We'll realize we can only serve God's kingdom purposes if we're motivated by God's love, trusting in God's power, and led by God's Spirit.

Don't expect everyone to go into the deep water with you. Some will, but many won't. It promises more than they can imagine, but it also requires more than they want to give. If we're committed to follow wherever God leads us, we can be sure he'll take us into the deep water. Peter wanted to experience more of Jesus, so Jesus told him to get out of the boat and walk on the water. Like many of us, Peter found the courage to take a step and experience a miracle, but like all of us, he had trouble staying on top. For the rest of his life, Peter never forgot the importance of answering Jesus' call and taking a bold step of faith.

When opportunities to serve God come, remember that Jesus gave his all for you. When you encounter troubles, remember he's with you in the storm. When you feel like giving up, remember that Jesus is the same yesterday, today, and forever. Your experience of the grace and greatness of God transforms you from the inside out. Knowing him gives you the love and strength to engage difficult people and difficult issues instead of caving in or running away. No retreat . . . no excuses. Keep holding the hand that has reached out to you, and stay the course.

THINK ABOUT IT . . .

Remember that tenderness and tenacity are essential if we want to go into the deep water of knowing, loving, and serving God.

1. What are some common excuses people give for bailing out on God or settling for a superficial commitment to him and his kingdom?

2. How is Jesus' summons to "take up your cross" both a threat and a promise? How have you answered this summons?

3. How would you describe the relationship between our experience of the tenderness of God and our tenacity to live for him?

Lord Jesus, you didn't make any excuses. You fulfilled the Father's will and served us to the point of death. Give me the heart, the wisdom, and the courage to follow you wherever you lead me.

GO DEEPER . . .

1. What does Rom. 8:15-17 say about your identity in Christ?

2. How does Matt. 25:14-30 describe God's purpose for you?

3. How does Heb. 13:20-21 show you how to stand strong and stay on track?

ENDNOTES

1   Gallup Poll on Marriage, www.gallup.com/poll/117328/marriage.aspx

2   "2015: Year in Review: Barna's Top 10 Findings in 2015," December 16, 2015, www.barna.org/research/culture-media/article/year-in-review-2015#.VpPiHihRZnE

3   Daniel Yankelovich, *New Rules: Searching for Fulfillment in a World Turned Upside Down* (New York: Random House, 1981).

4   These four responses to culture are adapted from Richard Niebuhr, *Christ and Culture* (New York: Harper & Row, 1975).

5   "With Same-Sex Decision, Evangelical Churches Address New Reality," Michael Paulson, *New York Times*, June 28. 2015.

6   N.T. Wright, *Simply Jesus* (New York: HarperOne, 2011), p. 5.

7   Viktor Frankl, *Man's Search for Meaning* (Beacon Press, 2006), p. 86.

8   C.S. Lewis, *Mere Christianity* (New York: HarperCollins, 2015 ed.), p. 120.

9   Saint Augustine, *Confessions*, (Lib 1,1-2, 2.5,5: CSEL 33, 1-5).

10 "The Lyubov Orlova—A Russian Ghost Ship Drifting Through International Waters," Sobify, www.sobify.com/the-lyubov-orlova-a-russian-cruise-ship-drifting-through-international-waters/

11   Cornelius Plantinga, Jr., "Sin: Not the Way It's Supposed to Be," Christ on Campus Initiative, 2010, tgc-documents.s3.amazonaws.com/cci/Pantinga.pdf

12   Stephen Charnock, *The Complete Works of Stephen Charnock, Vol. 4* (Amazon Digital Services, Inc., 2010), p. 199.

13   D.A. Carson, *For the Love of God*, Volume 2 (Wheaton, IL: Crossway Books, 2006), selection for January 23.

14   "Why does salt make (almost) everything taste better?" Kevin Liu, *Science Fare*, July 10, 2013, http://sciencefare.org/2013/07/10/why-does-salt-make-almost-everything-taste-better/

15   Biologically speaking, salt (sodium) plays a major role in human health. It not only feeds nutritional mineral elements to our cells, it also dissolves, sanitizes and cleanses toxic wastes from our system. It is this latter function that makes salt such a healing substance. All classic biology textbooks refer to salt as the cleanser of bodily fluids. (http://altmedangel.com/salt.htm)

16   Timothy Keller, *Generous Justice* (New York: Dutton, 2010), p. 4.

17   *Festival Letters*, quoted by Eusebius, *Ecclesiastical History* 7.22, 1965 ed.

18   Rodney Starks, *The Rise of Christianity* (HarperOne: New York, 1996), pp. 7, 73-94.

19   For more on salt-curing meat, go to Morton Salt's site: www.mortonsalt.com/for-your-home/culinary-salts/meat-curing-methods

20   Peter Haas, *Pharisectomy: How to Remove Your Inner Pharisee and Other Religiously Transmitted Diseases.* (Springfield, MO: Influence Resources, 2012).

21   "Why Loneliness May Be the Next Big Public-Health Issue," Justin Worland, *Time*, March 18, 2015, time.com/3747784/loneliness-mortality/

22 For more on the differences in the generations, see research
    by LifeWay: "Becoming Family: Understanding Generations
    in the Church," Jeanine Bozeman, www.lifeway.com/Article/
    Church-library-ministry-becoming-family-understanding-
    generations-in-the-church

23 "5 Lies Millennials and Baby Boomers Believe about Each Other,"
    Mark Hill, Cracked, December 2, 2015, www.cracked.com/
    blog/5-lies-millennials-baby-boomers-believe-about-each-other/

24 "Friendship," Timothy Keller, Redeemer Presbyterian Church,
    May 29, 2005.

25 Dietrich Bonhoeffer, *The Cost of Discipleship* (New York:
    Touchstone, 1959), pp. 44-45.

USING *STAY THE COURSE* IN GROUPS AND CLASSES

This book is designed for individual study, small groups, and classes. The best way to absorb and apply these principles is for each person to individually study and answer the questions at the end of each chapter then to discuss them in either a class or a group environment.

Each chapter's questions are designed to promote reflection, application, and discussion. Order enough copies of the book for each person to have a copy. For couples, encourage both to have their own book so they can record their individual reflections.

A recommended schedule for a small group or class might be:

WEEK 1

Introduce the material. As a group leader, tell your story of finding and fulfilling God's dream, share your hopes for the group, and provide books for each person. Encourage people to read the assigned chapter each week and answer the questions.

WEEKS 2–9

Each week, introduce the topic for the week and share a story of how God has used the principles in your life. In small groups, lead people through a discussion of the questions at the end of the chapter. In classes, teach the principles in each chapter, use personal illustrations, and invite discussion.

PERSONALIZE EACH LESSON

Ask people in the group to share their responses to the questions that meant the most to them that week. Make sure you personalize the principles and applications. At least once in each group meeting, add your own story to illustrate a particular point.

Make the Scriptures come alive. Far too often, we read the Bible like it's a phone book, with little or no emotion. Paint a vivid picture for people. Provide insights about the context of people's encounters with God, and help those in your class or group sense the emotions of specific people in each scene.

FOCUS ON APPLICATION

The questions at the end of each chapter and your encouragement to group members to be authentic will help your group take big steps to apply the principles they're learning. Share how you are applying the principles in particular chapters each week, and encourage them to take steps of growth, too.

THREE TYPES OF QUESTIONS

If you have led groups for a few years, you already understand the importance of using open questions to stimulate discussion. Three types of questions are *limiting*, *leading*, and *open*. Many of the questions at the end of each lesson are open questions.

Limiting questions focus on an obvious answer, such as, "What does Jesus call himself in John 10:11?" They don't stimulate reflection or discussion. If you want to use questions like these, follow them with thought-provoking, open questions.

Leading questions require the listener to guess what the leader has in mind, such as, "Why did Jesus use the metaphor of a shepherd in John 10?" (He was probably alluding to a passage in Ezekiel, but many people don't know that.) The teacher who asks a leading question has a definite answer in mind. Instead of asking this kind of question, you should just teach the point and perhaps ask an open question about the point you have made.

Open questions usually don't have right or wrong answers. They stimulate thinking, and they are far less threatening because the person answering doesn't risk ridicule for being wrong. These questions often begin with "Why do you think . . .?" or "What are some reasons that . . .?" or "How would you have felt in that situation?"

PREPARATION

As you prepare to teach this material in a group or class, consider these steps:

1. Carefully and thoughtfully read the book. Make notes, highlight key sections, quotes, or stories, and complete the reflection section at the end of each chapter. This will familiarize you with the entire scope of the content.

2. As you prepare for each week's class or group, read the corresponding chapter again and make additional notes.

3. Tailor the amount of content to the time allotted. Encourage people to study the "Going deeper" passages and invite them to share what they've learned.

4. Add your own stories to personalize the message and add impact.

5. Before and during your preparation, ask God to give you wisdom, clarity, and power. Trust him to use your group to change people's lives.

6. Most people will get far more out of the group if they read the chapter and complete the reflection each week. Order books before the group or class begins or after the first week.

ABOUT THE AUTHOR

Widely known as "Pastor Choco," Wilfredo De Jesús is the Senior Pastor of New Life Covenant Church in Chicago. Under Pastor Choco's leadership, New Life Covenant is the largest church in the Assemblies of God Fellowship.

Wilfredo was born and raised in Chicago's Humboldt Park community. When he was seventeen years old, he received Jesus as his Lord and Savior at a small Pentecostal Spanish-speaking church in the community. From that moment, his life was forever transformed.

He remained in that same little church for over twenty years before he was appointed Senior Pastor in July 2000. Since then, the church has grown from a weekly attendance of 120 to 17,000 globally through church plants and more than 130 ministries reaching the most disenfranchised—the brokenhearted, poor, homeless, prostitutes, drug addicts, and gang members.

Rev. De Jesús has been instrumental in the development of several community-based programs such as New Life Family Services, which operates a homeless shelter for women with children. Some of the church's other vital ministries include the Chicago Master's Commission, an intensive discipleship program for college-age students, and the Chicago Dream Center which offers various programs and services to assist individuals and families to move toward self-sufficiency and to overcome poverty and its ill effects.